Tasha Tudor's
GARDEN

Tasha Tudor's
GARDEN

Text by Tovah Martin
Photographs by Richard W. Brown

Houghton Mifflin Company
Boston   New York

For information about permission
to reproduce selections from this book, write to
Permissions
Houghton Mifflin Company
215 Park Avenue South
New York, New York 10003

Library of Congress Cataloging-in-Publication Data
Martin, Tovah.
Tasha Tudor's garden / text by Tovah Martin ; photographs by Richard Brown.
p.   cm.
ISBN 0-395-43609-5
1. Gardening – Vermont. 2. Tudor, Tasha – Homes and haunts – Vermont.
I. Brown, Richard, 1945-   II. Title.
SB455.M369   1994
635.9'092 – dc20   94–7886
CIP

SFE 20 19 18 17 16 15 14 13 12 11
Printed in Italy

Book design by Susan McClellan

Color separations by Sfera - Printing by Sfera

Tasha Tudor's calendars, cards, lithographs, and books are available from
Jenny Wren Press, P.O. Box 505, Mooresville, Indiana 46851

Contents

A Garden Lost in Time

❧

I MET TASHA TUDOR the same way that most people make her acquaintance. When I was very young, my favorite aunt paid a visit, and since she worked for a printing house and since we shared a flowing correspondence, she brought a gift of Tasha Tudor stationery. If my aunt hoped for a return note on that writing paper, I am afraid she was sadly disappointed, because I refused to part with a single sheet of it. Instead, I kept the box squirreled in my desk until the day it accompanied me to college, where all the blank sheets, but only the blank sheets, were used to write letters home. Then, when I came to work at Logee's Greenhouses in Connecticut, it followed me here. I still have that box of stationery, just slightly yellowed by time, tucked in the top drawer of my desk.

I had been at the greenhouses only a few months when I heard a rumor that Tasha Tudor was about to walk through our front door. As you can well imagine, I was floored. It shouldn't have come as such a shock, really. After all, I was well aware of Tasha's reputation as a keen plantswoman. But when I caught wind of her visit, I began walking on air. I brought out my stationery to show off and collected a pile of books to be autographed, but Tasha would have none of it. She was more interested in seeing our collection of dwarf fuchsias. And that, in a nutshell, has been the essence of our relationship ever since.

Occasionally we talk about art, every once in a while we discuss literature or animals, but usually Tasha and I spend our time sharing observations on plants. She knows far more than I, of course, but she politely asks me questions every now and then about camellia cultivation or whether auricula primroses should be given a sunny window during the winter. Undoubtedly Tasha wants to fool me into imagining that I'm contributing some-

> " I haven't any modesty when it comes to my old roses. They're heavenly. "

thing of value to our relationship. After all, she knows full well that auriculas will tolerate only filtered sun, and she could tell me a thing or two about the whims and fancies of camellias.

Over the years I've been up to see Tasha's garden on numerous occasions, but never quite as often as I'd like. Whenever she calls to lure me over, I'm sorely tempted to hop in the car and brave her steep driveway to spend a few blissful days smothered in flowers and plied with good food. Occasionally, I succumb and head northward. On one such visit I happened to arrive on the same day as Richard Brown, who came out from behind his lens for just a moment to shake hands and mention that the poppies were incredible this year – and had I seen the six-foot-tall foxgloves in the secret garden? That sealed our friendship forever.

Tall and stately, with a disarming smile frequently punctuated by a ready and soothing laugh, Richard is a modest man fond of rural pursuits. "Richard is every inch a gentleman," Tasha often says, and that's her highest compliment. He first made Tasha's acquaintance while photographing her greenhouse for a magazine years ago. "I did an abysmal job," Richard assures everyone who asks, but he's always ruthlessly critical of his own work. "No, really," he'll insist. "I was so much in awe of Tasha and so flabbergasted by her garden that I didn't do my best photography on that first visit." But from that day on, Richard has been visiting Tasha, driving down from his secluded farm in the best and worst weather to capture Tasha and her

garden in all their moods. Even he will admit that sometimes he has succeeded in his mission.

A trip to visit Tasha cannot be taken lightly, and she'll gladly warn you of the pitfalls when you first consider making the excursion. After you've climbed the very steep and frightfully perilous road to her mailbox, there's a long driveway to navigate. Only the very brave attempt the feat, and Tasha wouldn't have it any other way. When the worst of the potholes have been left in the dust, you finally reach a spreading meadow where lupines bow and curtsy. The drive cuts a swath right through it; for a few memorable moments you're lost in a crowd of purple spires, and then the house comes into view.

TASHA'S HOUSE looks as if it has always commanded the crest of her hill, and that's exactly the impression that Tasha wants to convey. Inside and out, it seems very timeworn indeed, accented by all the little crannies and imperfections that usually accumulate only with use and companionship. But in truth, Tasha's son Seth built the house for his mother only twenty-one years ago, and the intentionally low-slung doorways and uneven floorboards were installed at that time. If Tasha searched the world over, I don't think that she could have found a suitable house to fit all her numerous qualifications, and she certainly wouldn't have

---

Summer mornings find Tasha puttering around her garden, searching for flowers to fill bouquets. In June, it's the peonies ("I prefer the big bomb types") and old roses that most often come inside to sit in front of her easel.

found it waiting on exactly the right spot, conveniently near her son and his family. So she sent Seth to measure a 1740 farmhouse in Concord, New Hampshire, that caught her fancy, and he used all his consider able carpentry skills to recreate it on the plot of land next door to his cottage.

Although Tasha likes to let the house's apparent age fool you at first, she's quite willing to reveal the ploy after she has had her fun. Then she slides neatly into a little maternal boasting, and in this case it's well deserved – building Tasha's dream house was definitely a feat. Seth is every bit as reluctant as his mother to embrace the twentieth century, so only hand tools were employed during the construction of Tasha's home. He

Tasha grows some flowers, such as the parrot tulips above, just for painting, while others, like the stately delphiniums sitting right outside her bedroom window, are cultivated to enhance the view.

Tasha is fond of vignettes, such as the crab-apple and daffodil scene above and the drama that unfolds on her upper terrace (previous page).

raised the ten-by-ten beams for the barn by hand, using cranes to share the burden; he spent evenings whittling pegs to secure the posts. The result looks for all the world like the 1740 farmhouse Seth copied, except the floor plan was reversed to fit the lay of the land, because as Tasha explains, "Seth didn't know how to use dynamite."

As soon as the barn was completed, Tasha moved in. "I lived in the barn for a year with-out any heat," she will let slip, with just a tinge of Yankee stoicism in her voice. In the meantime, Seth worked on the house with its labyrinth of snug rooms. When it was com-pleted and brand-new, the Tudor home already seemed centuries old and very comfortable indeed.

I've visited Tasha in all sorts of weather, both bad and brilliant, and even when her mountaintop is drenched with sun, the house seems dark inside. So the garden is particularly sparkling when you step out the door and find it stretched in front of you. While your eyes adjust, you see only the nearest terrace, which unfolds like a pleasant dream in the depths of night. It seems surreal,

When the weather is conducive, Tasha cajoles a friend or relative into posing in the garden. In a pinch, she sits a corgi or a cat among the blooms.

like a splendid mirage, and sometimes I wonder if the house was made purposefully dark just to bestow the garden with that glistening effect. Knowing Tasha and her cunning tricks, I wouldn't put it past her.

Tasha will tell you that the garden wasn't a planned affair. "It just sort of grew – like Topsy," she always says. Well, I happen to know that the terraces were actually carefully drawn out, and I've also heard that Jim Herrick, the craftsman who laid the big, flat stones, was given rather specific instructions on their placement. Those instructions were followed to the inch, but apparently the mason refused to leave pockets for plants. "If he were building those terraces today, I would have insisted on the plant pockets – you can be certain of that," Tasha still fumes. And I have no doubt that nowadays Jim Herrick wouldn't come out of their little disagreement so victorious.

With or without plants tucked between the

masonry, the terraces are ingenious, and so are all the plantings that followed. Long before I ever turned into Tasha's driveway, I had a feeling of what the garden must look like from the illustrations in her books. Being a proper Yankee, Tasha puts her garden to good use. On any given day you'll find her out there deeply immersed in a watercolor, totally absorbed in the task of capturing each detail of flora and mood on her easel. Tasha is the world's most industrious soul. Even in foul weather, she cuts snippets from the garden to bring indoors and use as inspiration for the borders that twine around her art. Or she coaxes some slender young friend or relative to don one of her vintage gowns and stand stock-still beside the hollyhocks while she regales everyone in earshot with a constant banter of stories, simultaneously documenting the event on sketching paper. When you know Tasha's garden, you discover it cropping up everywhere. You recognize the pansy baskets from her front door in the frontispiece of her latest book; you see the stand of delphiniums beside the goat barn recorded verbatim in a packet of stationery. Tasha's illustrations are like a garden diary. And Tasha's art allows this masterly gardener to parade her horticultural talents before the eyes of the world without forfeiting her privacy.

B UT ART IS NOT the garden's sole purpose. Tasha really is the quintessential Yankee, born and bred of good (if also quirky) New England

Tasha plies her visitors with a sinful spread of freshly picked fruits and vegetables, sometimes cooked into something delectable, sometimes served just as they were harvested.

stock. She comes from a long line of gardeners, like the uncle who took home so many prizes for his vegetables from the agricultural show each year that the judges finally barred him from competing. Not only is flower gardening in her blood, but kitchen gardening also comes quite naturally. Tasha must use what she cultivates. And she's most content, she absolutely glows with pride, when the fruits of her labor serve several purposes. Anyone will tell you that Tasha herself eats like a bird; one very sparing cup of soup lasts her most of the day. But she loves to go out into the garden, harvest some plump, ripe berries or an apronful of heirloom beans, collect a few fresh eggs from the coop and cook them into something scrumptious for a special guest. One reason she's so very fond of Richard is that, being such a tall and hard-working fellow, he can pack away quite an impressive serving. "Richard has asked for seconds," Tasha will announce with a triumphant twinkle in her eye.

So the garden earns its keep; it has its practical applications. But behind it all there's

an element of sheer fantasy. That's really the crux of Tasha's garden. The truth is, Tasha dearly loves each plant on her property; she adores every botanical for its own sake and speaks of them as if they were good friends. ("She's got a crown of buds, but she's been sulking in the dry weather," she will report of a favorite rose.) That's why Tasha can't abide watching her garden shiver without a proper snow cover; that's why she suffers a thousandfold in a drought. And perhaps that's why the garden always looks absolutely ravishing. Tasha likes to portray her friends in their very best light.

If Tasha's garden is a fantasy, its vision is rooted in the past. Although Tasha occasionally takes daring steps in her art, bravely trying new color combinations, she is essentially a retrospective person in all other aspects of her life. She prefers things with a history. In fact, she surrounds herself exclusively with tools, objects, and ideas from some earlier time. And that's really the essence of her garden as well. Her gardening skills were passed down through the family, so she practices many methods that were long ago forgotten by others. She plants varieties that would have been perfectly comfortable in a cottage garden several generations ago. The oldest roses,

The birdsongs from the garden are echoed by the cooing of Tasha's immodest fantail pigeons from the dovecote outside her window.

nearly extinct dianthus cultivars, heirloom narcissus dug from her mother's garden – these are the sorts of plant that find their home with Tasha. And all of Tasha's friends and acquaintances share an appreciation for old barns, old tools, and old clothes – those are the sorts of people that find their way to her door.

But most of all, we are bound together by a mutual respect for heirloom plants. Tasha lures her friends up to her garden with descriptions of seldom-seen primroses, peonies, lilies, and cinnamon pinks. And we come to discover those plants and more combined with inspired artistry. We wander among

Tasha must immerse herself in what she adores, and so when the garden is in full regalia, bouquets spill from every corner of the house.

divine daffodils framed in a lacework of crab apples and along forget-me-not paths disappearing into flowery glades. We become transfixed by this place lost in time. Then we tarry by lamplight until late in the evening, listening spellbound to stories of eccentric uncles with incredible green thumbs and chimney campanulas stretching nearly seven feet tall. We come to share the fantasy.

Prelude to Spring

IN A GARDEN tucked in the coldest pocket of southern Vermont, March is full of promises and false starts. For Tasha, it is the year's most trying period. Weary of winter, anxious to garden, fretting lest her azaleas perish from wind damage, Tasha spends most of late winter worrying about the snow. Strange as it might seem, snow is the crux of Tasha's little botanical paradise. And in early March, it seems as though the white blanket is always too sparse or too dense to suit Tasha's needs.

I will call her or she will ring me, and after a few polite inquiries into everyone's health and welfare, the conversation always turns to snow. I have visions of her holding the receiver gingerly away from her face so she can peer out the window and assess the snow level. "There's still a three-foot drift against the back door — you know, we've had to burrow a tunnel so we can escape." Or, "The snow began to melt yesterday and made such

> "There's a drift of snow at the back door, and snowdrops blooming at the front."

a crashing noise that Captain Pegler was moved to profanity for the first time since he's come to live with me." Captain Pegler is her parrot, bought from a sailor, and most of his days are spent repeating, "Naughty dog! Naughty dog!" in a voice remarkably akin to Tasha's. But occasionally, shades of his past career come out, usually when Tasha isn't within earshot, fortunately.

Although Tasha likes to boast of the snow at her back door and pretend to worry that it will never melt, she isn't really concerned. She becomes far more fretful when snow is sparse. "The snow has melted too early, and I fear that I've lost half the roses." An audible sigh is heard. "You should have seen my David Austin 'Heritage' rose last summer; it was a ravishing mass of cupped pink petals, each emitting the most fantastic scent. I heaped mounds of manure around the base, but one never knows with this weather, really . . ." Together, we ponder the

snow, its risings and fallings, its ups and downs. That's what friends are for.

In a normal year (but Tasha will quickly tell you that she hasn't experienced anything remotely akin to weather normalcy for the past ten years), the snow begins to recede noticeably by March. At long last Tasha can make some tentative excursions out into the bare gardens, with the corgyn (that's the plural of corgi, according to Tasha) romping at her side. Snowshoes are donned for the occasion, although Tasha might well be able to walk right on top of the ice-crusted blanket with no platform whatso-

ever; she weighs less than one hundred pounds. But so many layers of petticoats, skirts, shawls, sweaters, jackets, and whatnot are bundled under her cape that her frail figure appears quite plump as she trudges along, checking snow depths with a stick. Heaven knows what she hopes to ascertain during early March's maiden journeys round the borders and down the wildflower walks. Certainly the beds are

Although she can't truly detect winter's toll in March, Tasha must trudge out and check for signs of life in the garden, with corgyn in tow. For lengthier excursions, she dons snowshoes. Tasha never shovels her walks: "It's such a waste of energy. Instead, I just wade through it all."

still buried deep down. But she always returns from those treks quite buoyant – Tasha could see life in a dormant twig.

Fond of anything with feathers, Tasha has kept an ongoing record of the birds on her property. Her son Tom built this ingenious birdhouse out of an inverted flowerpot (left). One of the fowl in residence, a stray rooster, is scooped up into Tasha's caped arms and taken back to his coop (above).

Her friends spend most of March in a valiant effort to divert Tasha's attention from the weather, the snow (or lack thereof), the bitter temperatures, and the stalemate outside. It isn't such a difficult assignment, considering that cartons filled with seed packets arrive daily and must be dealt with posthaste. Those cartons and their contents furnish the grist for many long conversations and boasting sprees. Gardeners pride themselves on their staunchly held opinions, and Tasha holds her botanical prejudices

*When the snow finally melts
in sunny patches, the leaves of a few
tender bulbs breaking soil are revealed.
On the outskirts of the garden stands an oak
planted from an acorn that Tom
collected on one of his journeys.*

---

particularly strongly and dearly. Not only does she have her favorite flowers, such as hollyhocks and pansies, but not just any hybrids will do – it must be single holly-hocks and lavender pansies. I pity the poor feckless soul who might unwittingly praise the racy orange-and-purple pansy 'Jolly Joker' in Tasha's presence; he's

bound to hear a tirade of insults on the subject.

I'M QUITE CERTAIN that Tasha spends every winter evening huddled close to the toasty fireplace with her reading spectacles perched on the edge of her nose, poring over every seed catalogue and gardening book she can lay hands on. Perhaps she has spotted an irresistible pink brugmansia in a new book from Britain, or maybe she has happened upon an heirloom dianthus in a magazine photo, and the hunt is on. Tasha invariably has a "want list" of impossible-to-find plants and seeds that she simply must obtain. And that's where the inherent Tudor combination of wile, charm, and dogged determination comes in handy. When Tasha is in hot pursuit, heaven and earth will be moved if they stand between her and the seed she seeks. I doubt that she always finds all the choice plants that have caught her eye. But if Tasha hasn't secured every last variety she desires, it isn't for lack of trying. She orders from commercial seedsmen as well as serious hobbyists throughout Europe. She sends heart-rending pleas to friends both domestic and foreign, enlisting their help in the search. Carefully wrapped parcels of seed, plants, and pots follow Tasha home whenever she travels.

By March, the seed should be in her possession and ready for sowing. If not – if all her efforts to ferret out a favorite old variety fail – there's always Agway down the road. Even there she has found some treasures – she insists that Agway carries the most fragrant, most colorful sweet peas available. When her sweet peas are going full blast with a cheerful confection of vivid blues, pinks, salmons, and purples on stalwart vines, no one would challenge her claim.

BUT TASHA could never survive solely on the promise of future blossoms. During winter, the little greenhouse tucked on the top of the hill nurtures her soul and keeps the vase in front of her sketchbook well stocked with flowers. Every day, no matter how busy she happens to be, Tasha makes her way through the labyrinth connecting the house to the greenhouse and waters the plants blossoming inside. "If I weren't an illustrator, I'd be a greenhouser, just like you," Tasha often assures me in midwinter. And I suspect that the comment is not mere flattery. Tasha spends a lot of time fussing over the plants that reside under glass. And March is definitely their shining moment.

Of all the plants in the greenhouse, the camellias particularly appeal to Tasha. Fond of delicate colors and dramatic choreography, she has amassed a collection of the fluffiest, fullest, most divine camellias you can possibly imagine. Now, quite mature bushes jostle one another for space, stretching tall, shiny-leaved branches, nearly touching the glass. In March, Tasha often returns to the house bearing a covered basket of camellia blossoms tucked under one arm to arrange and rearrange in pewter bowls. In the depths of winter, those neatly snipped, fluffy-petaled flowers beg to have their likeness captured in watercolors, and Tasha is pleased to oblige. The japonicas and the reticulatas with their soft nest of stamens act as artist's models, but the more fragile and less plentiful sasanqua camellias remain in the greenhouse, suffusing the cool air with their delicious perfume, greeting Tasha with a rush of color and aroma when

Tasha spends evenings by the fire with a corgi puppy sitting comfortably in her lap. Camellias collected from the greenhouse lie where she can easily admire their splendor.

she first pushes the door open to slip inside.

Beneath the camellias, the ground is carpeted with an ocean of Cape primroses (*Streptocarpus*), all sending up dainty trumpets in pinks and lavenders. These mingle with an occasional stem of taller paperwhites, strategically placed to heighten the prevailing drama and aroma.

In March, the carefully orchestrated camellia scene is joined by a chorus of cool-loving semitropicals in full splendor. The orange jasmine (*Murraya exotica*), brought in from its summer sojourn outside, bears clusters of powdery cream blossoms that send their fragrance into every nook and cranny. A pair of clivias send up plump umbels of orange buds, a Canary Island broom (*Cytisus canariensis*) is smothered in anise-scented yellow blossoms, and above it all, a very old acacia holds sprays of wispy yellow blossoms. In one corner, wooden florist benches balance a colorful grouping of Tasha's primroses and blooming pelargoniums, ready to go into urns when summer finally arrives. Every other spare foot of space is taken with tender rosemary standards and potted herbs, awaiting the moment when they will again be wheelbarrowed outside into the garden. It's a crowded affair, filled to bursting with the ever-increasing repertoire of Tasha's tender

Tasha favors the japonica camellias, with their fluffy pompoms of blushing flowers. She has in her collection a medley of formal rose forms as well as a few reticulatas, each with a powdery nest of yellow stamens.

favorites. And yet, in March, it is certainly heaven under glass for Tasha and anyone brave enough to pay a visit.

THE TIME OF YEAR that Vermonters refer to as "mud season" comes in the beginning of April and prevents the delivery people from bringing parcels of plants and seeds directly to Tasha's door. Her road twists its way through a generous mile of unpaved scenery, and is difficult to navigate even in the best of conditions. During mud season, it is simply impassable. So for a few long weeks in April, the artist is entirely stranded.

The antics of the delivery people perturb Tasha no end. She calls her friends, warns them not to pay a visit, and describes the latest standoff with the UPS man. But besides nettlesome delays in the receipt of botanical shipments, being marooned on her mountaintop bothers Tasha very little in April. At last she can poke into the ground and check the winter's toll on her borders. At last she can collect twigs, cones, and other findings from outdoors and bring them triumphantly inside to pose in front of her easel. At last she has tangible, reassuring proof that her garden is alive, well, and ready to bloom another year.

During mud season, Tasha takes up the carpets in the parlor so the corgyn won't tread dirt all over their antique fibers, and she never ventures out herself unless shod in knee-high lime green wellies. They make a most impressive sloshing noise, punctuating each footfall as she trudges through the quagmire, toting buckets down to the goats, wheeling barrows around her borders.

Most years, there's still some dingy snow on the ground in April, but nonetheless, a few early bulbs manage to poke out of clearings here and there. These are the first inklings of spring, strategically planted on the quick-thawing southerly slope of the hill. Snowdrops, crocuses, scillas, and chionodoxas are tucked along the footpaths of frequent travel to surprise Tasha as she goes about her chores. Later in spring, when more exciting things

Despite the weather, the chores must be done. "The girls" – Tasha's milking goats – stay in the barn connected to her living quarters. However, when Bucky is in residence, he dwells downhill (and downwind) from the house. On the way to taking him his dinner, Tasha checks for sprouting bulbs and sometimes finds a few brave chionodoxas peeking up.

happen, Tasha will dismiss all these "minor bulbs" with an impatient wave of the hand. In retrospect, they always seem insignificant to her. But in April, I suspect, they are of the utmost importance.

The minor bulbs are sprinkled about capriciously, in an offhand manner, but they are conspicuously absent from the terraced

beds around the house. The reason that bulbs fail to appear anywhere near stone walls has to do with Tasha's scheme to foil the hordes of "chippy hackees" (known as chipmunks to the rest of us) that frequent the place. Although Tasha isn't greatly troubled by voles or mice, she is plagued by several extended families of mischievous chipmunks, who would gladly live on a steady diet of tulip bulbs if only it were possible. The corgyn, it seems, have been fed too many shortbread tidbits to care about chasing chipmunks. And Minou,

Tasha's lazy one-eyed cat, gave up hunting long ago in favor of snoozing in some soft, warm spot.

Tasha tucks vases of the French pussy willows that I've sent her in the pantry window, where she and Captain Pegler, the parrot, can watch their progress. "And have you ever tried rooting slips of herbs in the glass with the willow stems? Why, they root like a charm."

ALTHOUGH APRIL might hold just enough promise to lure Tasha on, it's still a month dominated by flowers grown indoors. In April, Tasha has been known to tote anything botanical and mobile into her house to admire on the windowsill. The stone steps of the cellar are crammed with antique pots planted thickly with paper-whites, 'Tete-à-Tete' narcissus, 'Minnow' narcissus, tulips, lily-of-the-valley, and crocus being fooled into thinking that winter is a brief and mild affair. Tasha never starts her forced bulbs early, but invariably waits until winter has firmly set in and the garden outdoors is entirely finished. When Christmas is over and Easter is imminent, the bulbs begin to bloom and are trundled upstairs in relays to extend the drama as long as possible. Every two weeks another armload of pots showing only a few tenuous sprigs of growth is set on windowsills, where Tasha can watch the budding progress and savor their instant of glory. In the cooler corners of the house, in the alcove leading into the weaving room, and in Tasha's bedroom, these spring flowers hold their splendor for several weeks before dropping petals.

Bulbs are not the only flowers forced on Tasha's windowsills. During her excursions round the fields and down the wildflower walks, Tasha often cuts some whips to force into blossom. Forced birch tops are the

Tasha insists that she didn't plant crocuses beneath her flowering crab apples; it was the work of the voles ("or perhaps the squirrels, one never knows"), who carried off the bulbs from elsewhere and made some lovely artwork. Spreading manure, however, falls strictly within Tasha's domain, and she spends the spring negotiating with neighbors for truckloads.

traditional base for the Tudor Easter egg tree. She cuts them in late winter, plunges the tips into a jug of charcoal and water, and by Easter they're clothed in a swath of dainty greenery. Although there isn't a forsythia to be found on Tasha's property ("They're too suburban for my garden," she'll sniff), friends bring her branches to force in April, and she's genuinely grateful for the spark of color. Every year without fail I send Tasha a swag of long, soft French pussy-willow branches cut from the forty-foot bush in our back yard. Last year she announced that the branches had rooted and were being babied in her nursery of fledgling shrubs. "But I have no intention of allowing mine to reach the heights that yours have attained," she chides.

Forced bulbs and branches are little contrivances to keep Tasha preoccupied during April, but primroses are another matter entirely. Of all Tasha's burning passions,

primroses rank among the most ardent. Tasha belongs to only two societies, the Welsh Corgi League and the Primrose Society. Although she rarely attends the meetings, she has kept her membership current to receive the seed list. By autumn, she has usually amassed a fairly formidable collection of flats sown to primrose seeds. The seed is sprinkled lightly over fine soil, the flat is given a good soaking from below, it's tucked under the grapevine on the back porch and covered over, "and then I just forget it until spring, when the

seedlings begin to germinate like Topsy."

As always, Tasha holds strong opinions on primroses. "The 'Pacific Giants' are too

Tasha is almost as proud of her pots as she is of her collection of plants. In all sizes and depths, they can provide just the right footing for each botanical. Before she can really sink her hands into the soil outdoors, Tasha spends huge amounts of time fussing over the violets and primroses indoors.

garish, don't you think?" She prefers the Barnhaven types, with their deep, rich colors, and the 'Juliana' hybrids, with single blossoms sprinkled democratically among the leaves rather than one plump bunch of blooms. But she has been known to travel several hours to find a particularly choice variety. On one of my first visits, years ago, I brought an incredibly hardy, deep burgundy 'Cowichan' primrose from Kristian Fenderson, a fellow primrose aficionado. I do believe that it sealed our friendship instantly. Tasha treated that gift as if it were a nugget of solid gold and still proudly reports on its progress each spring. Auricula primroses ("my show auriculas," she calls them) are another favorite. And not just any show auriculas, mind you. Above all, Tasha prefers yellow-and-gray auriculas, "the ones with the powdery farina in the center, like the one you gave me years ago. If you ever find one again, I hope you'll remember that my birthday is in August," she says, only half in jest.

The little wonders that pop up in spring, like the snowdrops beside the arbor, receive quite a bit of attention in April and are carried inside as models for artwork. Those sprigs join the potted primroses in Tasha's bedroom and are shuffled from window to window as the sun moves around the house. "I wake up to my corgyn and primroses every morning," Tasha explains.

THE PRIMROSES sink their toes only into well-composted goat manure mixed with leaf mold and shoveled into Tasha's antique terra-cotta pots, which she carted home from visits to Britain. Tasha really comes into her own when on the trail of old terra cotta. First of all, she knows exactly what she wants – the depth, the height, and how the bulge should look in the center. Different pots are for different plants, of course, and primroses favor the taller variety with no rim whatsoever and a mouth about four inches in diameter. Tasha will breeze onto an old English estate, spy a pot stack somewhere tucked away, buttonhole the head gardener, and have him packing up thirty or forty pots before you can wink twice. "And I refuse to pay more than fifty pence for any of them," she will add, in the same no-nonsense tone she undoubtedly invoked during the bargaining process.

Perhaps Tasha doesn't mind being marooned in early April. But by the end of the month, she has just about lost her patience with the mud, the drizzle, and the grayness outdoors. "Well, you know what Mark Twain said," she will grumble with a frayed edge to her voice. "New England has nine months of winter and three months of bad sledding." Then she'll pull on her wellies, button up several layers of wool sweaters, pin a shawl on top of it all, and march outside to peek under the mulch and clear the pine boughs away from her sprouting bulbs.

The Garden Awakens

Although Tasha might take peeks and make promises earlier in the season, she doesn't actually lift mulch until May. Then all the boughs and debris that were carefully laid in November are raked up and carted off to reveal a fringe of emerging sprigs and tufts. It's truly astonishing and rather comforting to witness how rapidly a Vermont garden can progress from brown stubble to divine profusion.

There is so little bare ground left in Tasha's tightly planted beds that they spring into full-blown drama immediately. Tasha can begin boasting of her garden's splendor early in May, and she always does. "I shouldn't brag, but you should see my daffodils," she'll let slip to anyone who hasn't yet paid a spring visit. Or you might receive a seductive little note scribbled beside a quick sketch of a tulip or daffodil: "I'm terribly immodest, I know, but you must see my tulips, they've outdone themselves this year."

> " I believe in making a big splash, so I plant shocking amounts of tulip bulbs."

The truth is, when you go to pay a call, the garden far surpasses all Tasha's tantalizing descriptions. She isn't being immodest at all.

May begins as a frilly, lacy affair, like the antique gowns that Tasha keeps in her attic. Then the landscape rushes up into a confection of budding color garnishing the greenery. From that time on, things happen at such a brisk pace that Tasha is breathless to keep abreast. If ever there is a month when she thrusts aside sketching to devote full time and energy to the garden, that moment comes in May. Of course, the blooms of May were planned and planted in previous autumns, when Tasha braved the chilly, gloomy weather to slip quantities of bulbs into the soil, and besides receiving some strategic primping, the show cannot be improved this season. But gardeners are forever looking forward, and Tasha never wastes a minute idly admiring the fruits of her labor; she is always marching onward. A great deal of preparation must be performed in May if the rest of the season is to come off as hoped.

May is a time of rebirth not only in the garden; there's action in the barnyard as well. A new crop of frisky Nubian goat kids are careening pell-mell around the pasture, their floppy ears bouncing while they play king of

the mountain on tree stumps. Meanwhile, the coop is teeming with dozens of tiny chicks, no bigger than a minute, being marshaled around by protective hens. Gardeners, I have noticed, tend to harbor an affinity for fowl as well as flowers, and Tasha certainly has a soft spot for anything with feathers. She has kept bantams and guinea fowl on the property; once she used geese to chase off unwanted visitors, but the geese took to treading on her primroses and nibbling her water lilies, so she gave them away. Now she has a flock of white fantail pigeons that live in a dovecote above the back porch and parade in front of the bedroom windows by the hour, admiring their own reflections in the glass. In the coop are Mille Fleurs and a brigade of broody Cochin bantams, whose tiny eggs, exactly half the size of other chicken eggs, garnish Tasha's summer salads.

Tasha cannot resist sending to far-off hatcheries for French Faverolles or some other rare bird, and the chicks monopolize quite a generous chunk of her time. Of course, other folks might rear

Tasha's paths beg to be followed. A journey down this one is cushioned in forget-me-nots and daffodils. One of Tasha's oversize bleeding hearts waits along the way.

poultry without spending more than a minute or two daily at the task, but not Tasha. She outright refuses to raise her chicks under heat lamps. Instead, they are given the luxury of crocks frequently refilled with hot water and wrapped in towels to huddle around when nights are chill. Later, when they venture out, Tasha rushes around gathering them up in her apron at the first droplet of rain, to hie them safely indoors and hand-dry each chick whose fluff became damp. For their part, the chicks repay that fine upbringing by gobbling down grubs in the garden and keeping the soil neatly scraped of weeds. Needless to say, "the birdies" aren't permitted in the borders in spring, when seedlings are sprouting everywhere. And to protect the primroses that line the front of the house, Tasha's grandson, Winslow, gathers hundreds of saplings every few years and weaves a short wattle fence, using no nails whatsoever, just like the fences his great-grandmother wove when Tasha was a child.

The birds and the bulbs are the prima donnas in May. Not just a few bulbs – thousands of them. "I believe in making a big splash," Tasha will confide, as if we hadn't noticed. Her philosophy is most evident in spring, when massive drifts of daffodils and other bulbs

dance and bow in the breeze. When Tasha buys bulbs, she does it in quantities of no less than a hundred ("I order shocking amounts," she will assure you), and she puts a few hundred in as fillers each fall to boost the already ravishing display. She started many years ago by purchasing several of the daffodil collection called The Works from White Flower Farm (in fact, their catalogue now features a splashy photograph of Tasha's barnside with The Works performing in full sail). The collections arrived one dismal autumn day when the road was absolutely hopeless, so she loaded the box of two thousand bulbs onto her wheelbarrow and trundled it down to the lower field to plant beneath a grove of crab apples bent with character. Then she dug trenches eight inches deep, sprinkled some fertilizer on the bottom, and spread a dozen or more bulbs in each ditch. In late autumn every year, Steve Davie, a neighbor who lends a hand in his spare time and sings Welsh ballads at Tasha's midsummer fling, takes out his scythe and cuts the grass in the daffodil field with broad, sweeping strokes. And every year the daffodils are fruitful and multiply until the lower field is an enthusiastic rhapsody in yellow and white.

The crux of Tasha's cottage garden is repetition, so echoing colonies of daffodils are scattered here and there throughout the terraces. Unlike The Works, these clusters have a pedigree that Tasha knows; she can

---

With such a bounty of daffodils beneath the crab-apple grove, Tasha can easily cut bouquets. This one was gleaned from The Works. It stands in front of a charcoal portrait of Tasha's grandmother Louise Tudor when she was eight years old.

point out and tell a story or two about the canary-yellow 'King Alfred', the late-flowering double 'Cheerfulness', her delightfully fragrant *Narcissus jonquilla*, the dwarf 'Minnow' or 'Tete-à-Tete'. Always sentimental, she planted a generous clump of 'Irish Moon' on the grave when her beloved Irish wolfhound, Una, passed away, and it has flourished there ever since. But above all, Tasha is particularly proud of her mother's *Narcissus poeticus* 'Plenus', the oldest narcissus in cultivation, which she has dug up

Not far from the crab apples, a bleeding heart spreads its finely cut foliage and wands of flowers. Meanwhile, bouquets are tucked in every nook and cranny of the house. This one was composed for the benefit of Tasha's cinnamon and zebra finches.

and transplanted wherever she lived. It has one glaring fault – the sheaf that wraps each bud refuses to fall free and must be removed by hand – but Tasha patiently performs the service so the blossoms won't blast.

Tasha enjoys such a bounty of daffodils that she doesn't think twice before cutting blossoms to bring indoors. But the tulips are

less long-lived and thus more precious. Tasha fancies the way they look in a vase perhaps more than she values their profile in the garden, so most tulip buds are lopped off early in their career to fill bouquets. Needless to say, all the tulips on the premises are carefully color-balanced with just that purpose in mind.

Tulips are planted with the same generosity as daffodils, but they reside primarily in the upper border, well away from the stone walls and the greedy "chippy hackees." No living creature dares to eat daffodils, not even the ravenous goats, but tulip bulbs are apparently a delicacy few furry animals can resist. Since tulips tend to be a transient affair, especially when spring downpours shatter their petals, Tasha prefers the tightly furled types in gentle pastels. She has deliberately choreographed the display to extend the splendor and provide fillers for bouquets as long as possible. First off, there are the pinkish salmon 'Beauty Queen' and palest salmon 'Apricot Beauty', followed by 'Peerless Pink' and 'Elizabeth Arden', a stately pink Darwin tulip with a bluish flush. Later come true blue 'Lafayette' and butter-yellow

'Mrs. John T. Scheepers', matching the yellow alyssum and the late daffodils down below.

When asked if she isn't tempted by the new "perennial tulips," Tasha will cluck her tongue disapprovingly and dismiss them with

---

When friends arrive, especially petite friends, Tasha often disappears into the attic and returns with an antique gown that just might fit. In spring, vases of tulips complement the fantasy.

a wave of her hand. "Mine continue to bloom for seven years or more. Of course, the flowers become much smaller in later seasons, but they're lovely all the same." She's quite sure that the new "perennials" wouldn't possess the delicate nuances of color in 'Apricot Beauty' ("I've just ordered two hundred more") or 'Elizabeth Arden', and she's probably right.

To the artist, color is of the utmost importance. In May, her beds are a soft elixir of delicate shades – dawn pinks, palest mauves, lavenders, butter yellows (never garish sunray shades) beside a foil of lacy white. Patches of each hue are scattered and then repeated seemingly arbitrarily, but of course nothing here is arbitrary. And everything is offset by a filigree of freshly clothed leafy vines, like the golden hops by the porch laundry tub, and newly leafed shrubs, such as the mock orange and weigela. It's a gentle, melodious scene, meant not to send your head spinning but to tickle your senses and sensibilities instead.

Bleeding hearts also play a major role in the net of color cast over the garden. Tasha is immensely proud of her bleeding hearts, and with good reason. They are the envy of every visitor who happens to brush past their dangling flowers on the path. When in full swing, they stand four feet tall and have an equal girth, and shower countless blossoms. Not only do the common pink bleeding hearts display uncanny exuberance, but the rare pure white bleeding hearts are equally energetic. Their heft is certainly reason for comment, but the trait that totally confounds me is their ability to bloom nonstop throughout the season. To be sure, in mid-August Tasha's bleeding hearts don't drip with as many flowers as they do during spring's first spurt of vigor, but they still make a fairly respectable showing. Tasha herself can't explain the phenomenon, except to say rather smugly, "Perhaps they like it here."

The garden is veiled in diffuse color in springtime, when violets, alyssum, forget-me-nots, 'Apricot Beauty' tulips, and crab apples all come into splendor.

OTHER THAN THE SOFT SALMONS that play in the petals of some tulips, orange is not frequently found in Tasha's garden. The grand exceptions are her *Fritillaria imperialis*, the crown imperials that line the raised bed on the corner of the greenhouse, jutting tall and each holding a fiery cluster of nodding orange blossoms. These spectacular plants are extremely tender, yet Tasha manages to prod them along until they reach their splendid peak. "The silly things come up too early each year, and their tender shoots get nipped by the late frost. They droop pathetically next morning, but they straighten up by noon and seem none the worse for the freeze," she'll say casually, knowing full well that I'm green with envy. In Connecticut our crown imperials also lack the good sense to wait until danger of frost is past before sprouting, but ours invariably become gnarled and stunted as a result of their indiscretion.

The crown imperials might be a little out of character because of their glaring color, but they say a lot about Tasha as a gardener. She is forever tempted by a challenge. I guess that she has tried everything once. Some plants are later discarded as inappropriate, boring, or simply not conducive. Other plants remain because they have a history, they fit with the cottage scene, or they're just plain gorgeous. And a few plants are kept so Tasha can let slip every once in a while that she has succeeded at some feat that other gardeners find

difficult or impossible to achieve.

Although she entertains a few boast-worthy botanicals, these are far outweighed by favorites, which are welcomed in droves. Certainly forget-me-nots and Johnny-jump-ups are given free rein in the borders. For her part, Tasha prefers to call Johnny-jump-ups by the name her mother employed for these endearing little violas – lady's delight – and she always makes a tsking sound under her breath and corrects me when I address her plants improperly. First of all, she considers these wild pansies to be feminine, not masculine by any means. If I point out a rogue seedling with particularly pert markings and compliment it, she'll nod and agree: "Yes,

Tasha's crown imperials, Fritillaria imperialis, *are among the few raging orange flowers that she permits in her garden. In pansies, however, she can't abide the new orange-and-purple 'Jolly Joker', which is now in vogue. She prefers the more discreet monkey-faced types instead.*

she's got a lovely face." In Tasha's opinion, only noxious weeds are masculine.

Some gardeners might accuse Johnny-jump-ups (or whatever you choose to call them) and forget-me-nots of being slightly weedy in character, but not Tasha. Heaven help anyone who, imagining that he is doing Tasha a favor, thins out seedlings from the terraces. Tasha claims that she gives the lady's delight and myosotis a little selective curbing, but I've never seen her lay a finger on either of those wild-lings. Usually they are suffered to stay (and encouraged, I suspect). Forget-me-nots carpet the paths in plenitude, like a sea of raging purple, while Johnny-jump-ups interbreed with shameless fertility, scampering in and out every-where, shielding the ankles of taller per-ennials. Rather than having the deep royal purple shades that most gardeners let romp about, Tasha harbors a strain of stunning, muted lavender-and-yellow lady's delight with chubby-cheeked petals and saucy dark whiskers. The hue matches the myosotis perfectly, and they are quite a twosome, rushing along the ground.

But that's not all. By the end of the month,

Tasha keeps her own strain of Johnny-jump-ups, or lady's delight, as she calls them. "I've taken them with me wherever I've gone since my teens. I suppose they came from Scotland originally," she'll say. They just happen to match her favorite forget-me-nots perfectly.

the prevailing low-lying pale lavender is echoed in lilacs that hold their fragrant plumes at arm's length beside stone steps and beneath the parlor windows. There are several lilacs growing on the place. Beside the porch, framing and fragrancing the view toward the garden, is a statuesque old 'President Lincoln' with plump purple tresses nearly hidden behind the leaves. Only a few steps away, the double blossoms of 'Miss Ellen Wilmott' open like fluffy white clouds to shade the parlor. Then there's an enormous blue lilac perfuming the henyard; Tasha can't recall its name, but she'll assure you that she went out of her way to find a particularly fragrant variety, for obvious reasons. And a dense semicircle of deep purple lilacs intertwine their branches to hem in the secret garden that is off to the side of the front door.

THE LILACS add their leitmotif to the chorus of color, but the crab apples are the stars – they steal the scene. Inspired by Dorcas Brigham, a close friend and famed horticulturist who taught botany at Smith College, Tasha planted an orchard of these lovely trees at the bottom of her terraces and scattered a few elsewhere in the gardens. "Oh, you should see them by moonlight, when I look down from my bedroom window," she will say, with a far-off look in her eye. She planted more than a dozen crab apples, with staggered blooming times and different shades of flowers. Among her favorites are 'Red Jade', 'White Weeper', *Malus sargentii*, and especially 'Bechtel' ("Oh,

she's a late bloomer with blossoms like Bourbon roses – the envy of everyone who visits").

Since being planted, the crab apples have required very little care; they just seem to spread their skirts and perform with divine artistry. But Tasha fidgets nonetheless. "I wish I knew more about pruning," she says, sighing. "I do my best – I take off the suckers – but the crab apples deserve better." And then she calls up a week or two later and announces that she has found just the book on the subject, written by Lewis Hill, "who lives up in the northeast kingdom and knows all about our forbidding climate. I sleep with a copy of his book under my pillow and read it every night. Next January those crab apples

When May arrives, Tasha must often rush out to the barn to tend to her crop of Nubian kids. Meanwhile, the stonework of the terraces half disappears beneath creeping phlox, and lemon-yellow trollius comes up everywhere.

"I've forgotten exactly which crab apple this is,"
Tasha will say, donning spectacles to examine
the flowers more closely. "Possibly **hupehensis,** *I*
suppose." Beside it, a stand of comfrey is con-
fined by a stone wall. When a goat is under
the weather and refuses dinner, a few leaves
of comfrey soon set her straight.

are going to receive quite a proper pruning, I promise." And I certainly know Tasha well enough by now to envision her in snowshoes, wrapped in her red cape, loppers in hand, making very well calculated cuts.

B UT IN MAY the crab apples don't look as if they should be touched. They really are a sight to behold. And Tasha likes to make a lot of her flowering trees and shrubs, echoing their colors in the beds lying below the branches, contrasting them cleverly by scattering bloomers down below, playing them to the hilt. You see the artist's handiwork everywhere – in the blushing crab apple cushioned in creeping phlox and sweet rocket, and in the delectably aromatic mock orange enhanced by a blanket of pure white bleeding hearts. These are not the sort of accomplishments that Tasha can easily boast about. She can't very well lure you up to see her flowering crab apples or her lilac hedge fringed with forget-me-nots. Nonetheless, when you do come, it's bound to take your breath away. It's all part of the prevailing splendor.

Flowers in Profusion

THE TERRACES TEND TO predominate in Tasha's landscape, but the property is sprinkled with plenty of peripheral gardens as well. In fact, Tasha is forever dreaming up some ingenious upheaval – ripping this out, putting that in, moving something to the left or right. New gardens appear with astonishing regularity. Every season the plans for a little alcove are in the works, and Tasha is full of tales of shrubs being slipped into the soil just moments before a killing frost or holes being dug with pickaxes when plants arrive after the normal planting time. Tasha loves to maneuver, digging up half her roses and trundling them to some better spot where their glory will shine as never before. And she dotes on the planning process, cooking up wondrous follies. But her favorite pastime, it seems to me, is blazing paths that go nowhere in particular. I have always suspected that the idea for a path pops into Tasha's mind first,

> " I don't make proper flower arrangements; mine just grow, like the garden. "

and then a destination must be created.

Of course, the paths serve an important social function. Tasha is always sending visitors roaming while she fusses in the kitchen over biscuits or cornbread. "Now, you show yourself around the garden," she'll say, in a tone that leaves scant room for discussion, "while I prepare something to eat. Take that path and find the lily pond – it's high noon and you just might catch the flowers open. Let me know if the pond is low." So you are dispatched on a wandering journey down one of her meandering paths. The passage is absolutely enthralling, and you're soon lost in a series of nooks and crannies that you never explored before. You could certainly tarry forever and never retrace your steps to the farmhouse and tea if it were not for the aroma of fresh, warm cornbread wafting down from the kitchen, sent to lure you back.

Although she will never admit it, Tasha likes to devote her gardens and their connecting paths to themes. So there is a wildflower walk, which takes a very leisurely route down to the lily pond (that particular path, the longest on the property, is normally assigned to visitors when cornbread is in the oven, I've noticed); there's the secret garden, with its brief but seductive forget-me-not–lined walkway; and there's a path that flows down the hill from the greenhouse and then disappears into clouds of azaleas. Paths lead down to the goat barn, over to the neighbors, out to the pasture, and so forth. In fact, little spurs, digressions, and loops crisscross the property everywhere, but Tasha has her favorite rambles, and those walkways have received the most thoughtful frill of flowers to cushion the passage.

A s I said, not all of Tasha's paths have a clear purpose other than a fantastic little jaunt into the woods. The rhododendron walk, for example, doesn't really go anywhere. It starts out ambitiously enough, only to halt rather abruptly at a fallen pine, circle around, and return. That's Tasha's way of telling you that woody groves and wildflower glades are worth a visit and no further excuses are necessary. Of course, there are other attractions in addition to the azaleas. If you look off into the forest in June, just when the azaleas are in full tilt, you might catch a glimpse of Tasha's little cache of pink lady's-slipper orchids; "I counted thirty in bloom last year," she'll boast. Originally, they were scattered throughout the property, too

far from civilization to be appreciated on a regular basis. So she moved a few into the deep, light soil within eyeshot of the azalea walk, just close enough for observant visitors to see, but sufficiently off the beaten path to remain elusive. The hemlocks and pines that populate the grove provide ample shade, maintain the proper pH, and furnish the orchid roots with the mycorrhiza fungi they need to survive.

Apparently the lady's-slippers are perfectly content in their new location – so happy, in fact, that they've multiplied freely. Half naturalist, half gardener, Tasha takes the greatest pleasure in monitoring the progress of her wildflowers, and every season she proudly reports her tallies – twenty-five orchids one year, thirty orchids the next, and so on. She loves nature dearly just the way it is; after all, most of her 250 acres are left completely wild. And yet, in the places immediately surrounding her house, she likes to compose very deliberate flights of whimsy and beauty. She likes to play with nature.

You wouldn't expect Tasha Tudor to permit just any old azaleas onto her property, and

Often when Tasha is busy in the kitchen, she sends guests wandering among the cool pastels of her Exbury azaleas. Not far away, a bountiful beautybush, Kolkwitzia amabilis, *hums with industrious bees.*

sure enough, the azaleas lining her walk are Exbury hybrids of the finest pedigree. Even at that, several bushes that had the effrontery to blossom in "awful colors" have been dug up

The Exbury azaleas are a fairly new addition. Long before they arrived, Tasha was planting blooming shrubs. "During my first spring here, I wheelbarrowed in rhododendrons and three beehives, because you can't live without rhododendrons or honey, can you?"

and carted off to distant locations. In Tasha's opinion, "awful colors" are defined as blazing shades, such as the screaming magenta so common in azaleas. Some people might refer to that particular hue as "fuchsia," but Tasha never does. She counts fuchsias (the more tastefully colored hybrids, of course) among her favorite flowers and will hear no ill word spoken against them. Certainly, she cannot bear hearing fuchsia mentioned in the same breath as magenta azaleas, which clash with the prevailing color scheme.

What remains since Tasha whittled the azaleas down to only restful shades is a muted palette of dainty pastels. In front, a diffuse screen of creamy butter blossoms open forth. Behind them stands a lacework of peachy hues, and farther back in the distance are a few darker orange hybrids to give it all definition. In the gaps left vacant when certain azaleas were sent out of sight, Tasha has planted English bluebells (*Endymion non-scriptus*), whose navy-blue spires coincide nicely with the azaleas. Rocket also fills in wherever it finds an opportunity. "Originally, this was just a mess of wild periwinkle. But I put an end to that in short order, I can assure you," Tasha will say in the sort of stiff tone that might make any man, beast, or weed beat a hasty retreat.

JUNE IS WHEN Tasha makes her firmest efforts to lure friends up to see her horticultural handiwork. And sometimes she becomes a little overwhelmed with the response. "I was an innkeeper in my last life, I'm certain of it," she'll say with a sigh when there has been a constant flow of houseguests. But she basks in good company. In fact, she plans little fetes to give us an excuse to drive up. In early spring, as soon as the roads will

Headed for new pastures, a brigade of Nubian milkers wade through the sea of lupines in the meadow. Amanda, queen of the herd, must be led on a leash to keep the parade from straying.

permit, Tasha hosts a party complete with garlands of wildflowers strung everywhere. She keeps promising us a giant, streamer-laden maypole for young friends to dance around and braid, but so far she has been too busy gardening to construct such elaborate attractions.

On Midsummer's Eve, or as close as she can conveniently come to the summer solstice, Tasha sets a giant bonfire ablaze in the lupine meadow ("The lupines love the potash," she quickly explains to anyone who might accuse her of frivolity). The weather is invariably perfect for that enchanted affair staged in the big field under the stars. Purple spires sway to the fiddle music, the corgyn

Tasha keeps her own carefully selected strain of poppies from her mother's seed, which she sows religiously every year. She favors the sherbet shades, and is especially proud of those with a raspberry cast.

bounce around and race between everyone's legs, yipping in delight, and little children in flower-studded crowns giggle and chase. With a twinkle in her eye, Tasha boasts of how long into the evening she has danced, and I have no doubt that she leaves many young fellows weary and winded while she continues her merry pace.

The parties are only a pretext, of course,

because it's the gardens that Tasha really wants to show off. And in June the gardens are at their finest. In that month they become an impressive blend of the best of lingering spring and a touch of summer. The terraces are in full bloom, so filled with every cottage flower in high pomp that you could wander hour after hour down the slender stone steps, around this little jog, under that rose arbor, and between mounds of spilling ground covers without growing bored. You could just amble idly about, enjoying the scenery, thinking enlightened thoughts and sharing them with the corgyn, which accompany you everywhere you go, but Tasha wouldn't have it. The best visitors are those who pitch in and help, preferably performing some feat that she cannot quite manage herself nowadays.

TASHA IS AS STRONG as a team of oxen, but at ninety-five pounds, even she has her limits. Long ago, she discovered that visitors should not be permitted to weed. They invariably ravage the poppies and forget-me-nots unmercifully. Tasha must make that sort of decision herself, thank you. Although the omnipresent lettuce poppies might seem like pure accident to the casual visitor, they're really quite deliberate. Tasha has selected her own personal mix of raspberry and peach sherbet shades from seed saved since her mother's garden, decades ago.

If the poppies don't come up with sufficient abandon, well then, Tasha keeps a special cache of seeds to sprinkle around. Heaven help anyone who dares pull up a poppy.

Tasha much prefers for you to offer to dig a hole for a new shrub, perhaps, or maybe to wheelbarrow a load of manure to some far-flung patch in need of fertilization. Better still, clean the goat barn. Visitors who transport muck from one spot to the next or perform some other back-breaking deed become legends; they are heroes in tales that she repeats over and over again. In fact, strangers who have occasionally strayed onto the property have become firm friends when they show a ready willingness to help out. Tasha loves to tell of the sightseer who happened to find his way up her drive one fine May morning, saw her sowing the meadow with wildflower seed, stopped his car, and asked if she had seen Tasha Tudor in that neck of the woods. "He had me snagged," Tasha admits. "I said that I was the lady in question, but I informed him that I was far too busy sowing wildflower seed that day to entertain company. So he took the bag and sowed my whole field by hand in no time. The field is several acres wide, you know." Needless to say, the fellow received a generous helping of piping hot cornbread and a good long chat as compensation for his efforts.

If Tasha is busy in the kitchen, she often sends guests to fetch some fresh ingredients from the vegetable beds, knowing that the journey will take them past terraces bursting with iris, baby's breath, lady's mantle, and a chorus of other blossoms. Down below, poppies, lupines, swamp iris, and lady's delight (following pages) are in full voice. In spring, rhubarb is the delicacy most in demand.

The point is that Tasha, being a Yankee through and through, enjoys hard work, and she expects those around her to share her enthusiasm for physical labor. Every day you'll find Tasha toiling away, tidying this, planting that, keeping her gardens absolutely picture-perfect. The gardens might look as if they've been allowed to do whatever they desire, but that's part of the ploy. Beneath it all, there's a great deal of work to be done, and Tasha depends on some willing extra hands to get it all accomplished. Young and old, relatives and strangers alike are expected to add something of value to the gardens when they pass through. Tasha is much too polite to ask for favors, but she's not above letting slip some subtle hints.

AFTER YOU'VE COMPLETED your chosen task, there's always a treat in store. As everyone knows, Tasha is an incredibly good cook, and tea is her favorite meal. When she has rested briefly from her morning's labors, you'll find her in the kitchen with her glasses perched on the tip of her nose, deep in concentration, whipping up some wonderful hot-cross buns or butterscotch rolls. If you arrive in the pantry before the treat is ready, you're dispatched posthaste on some errand or other – Tasha accepts no help whatsoever in the kitchen. But the moment tea is ready and it's time to sit down and partake, she will hear of no delays.

Tea has been taken at several different locations since I've been visiting Tasha. For a while, we sat down under the honeysuckle and *Clematis tangutica* arbor in the middle terrace overlooking the peony garden. A wisteria vine snakes over the bench, but it never blossoms, because Tasha's garden is just too cold. The honeysuckle, however, holds forth from June until September, and the nodding yellow clematis blossoms kick in for the latter part of the season. It was a cozy place for tea, but Tasha had to load her fine china on a tray and balance it through some tight, vine-encased twists and turns to reach the spot, so nowadays she prefers to serve on the porch, within easy fetching distance of the pantry.

There's a little table out there on which Tasha sets some stupendous plant she wants to show off, like her chimney bellflower or a fuchsia standard. It invariably monopolizes most of the serving space and all of the conversation for the afternoon. If nothing show-stopping is in bloom, she arranges an absolutely incredible bouquet with all sorts of rarities from the woods. Tasha's rocker is close by, a few chairs are pulled up, and the young folks are offered a comfy spot on the steps. At teatime there's always a sunbeam warming the chairs, and after Tasha basks in the sun and luxuriates in the compliments on her cooking, she eases into a few good stories while

Perhaps because they are so mobile, and perhaps because Tasha likes the company of blossoms everywhere, even on the porch, she always grows some of her favorite plants in pots. When she sits down for tea, a foxglove or some other little extravaganza stretches its flower stalks by her side.

everyone sits spellbound and asks for seconds. Quite a few hours slip by before anyone wants to return to work again.

AFTER TEA has been drawn out as long as possible, everyone disperses until the evening chores. Late afternoon offers Tasha's favorite light for drawing, and you'll often find her set up in one of the gardens, drawing from nature. When she's deep in the throes of an illustration, Tasha really prefers not to be disturbed, so she has made special places to hide – although she never minds having a quiet friend or two by her side to keep her company. ("I'm not a temperamental artiste, you know," she'll say.) In June you'll often find her in the peony gar-

The secret garden will one day be dominated by the roses, no doubt. But for now the foxgloves reign supreme, with a little help from frequent and generous applications of manure tea.

den, perched on the long bishop's bench, pad in hand, flanked on either side by clouds of fluffy flowers.

O F ALL TASHA'S GARDENS, only the peony alcove nods politely in the direction of formality. It's a fairly strait-laced affair composed of two peony-packed beds cut down the middle by a grassy promenade leading right to the bench. If it appeared in anyone else's landscape, you would see it as a very serious composition indeed. But it's in Tasha's domain, so it has humor and perhaps a touch of parody as well. Although the peonies do a praiseworthy job of filling out their plot with no help at all from supporting cast, they're edged by a modest foil of purple verbena, added to hide any naked ankles. Asiatic lilies wait in the wings to take over the performance when the peonies bow out.

In peonies, Tasha favors the big bomb types. To hear her boast of this penchant might sound a bit out of character – explosives are not what we associate with Tasha – but when you see these particular peonies and their confusion of fluffy petals, it's easy to understand why she has chosen these flowers, despite their name. The bomb types hold their blossoms in perfect form for quite a few weeks unless a summer shower comes along

---

I have noticed that almost every flower is Tasha's favorite, or so she says when asked. But only a few flowers are so coveted that they warrant a garden of their very own. Peonies definitely tug at Tasha's heartstrings, and the peony garden testifies to their charms. The bomb types (opposite), such as 'Festiva Maxima', are especially favored.

and drenches the heads with water. Not to be undone by a few raindrops, Tasha rushes out as soon as the precipitation ceases and patiently shakes off each nodding flowerhead until it can hold its petals skyward again. Needless to say, she strives to prolong the enchantment and provide grist for illustra-

tions over many weeks, so the peony beds are carefully stocked with early, midseason, and late-flowering varieties. The garden opens with the fragrant white flowers of 'Festiva Maxima', followed by a profusion of equally white pompoms crowning 'Mother's Choice'. By late season, the garden has slipped into a cooler shade of tissue pink, when 'Nick Shaylor' and the fragrant 'Sarah Bernhardt' take over the show.

The peonies are Tasha's pride and joy. At one time they were skirted with a band of yews, but as they gained heft, Tasha fretted that the garden looked like a telephone booth, and so the hedge was summarily removed. Anyway, while the hedge was in place, you couldn't properly admire the peonies from the spot where Tasha takes afternoon tea, so it really did have to go. Every autumn the peonies are cut to the ground and the prun-

ings are burned to prevent the spread of disease. Then the garden is laid thick with a generous dressing of manure "as black as ink." That, in a nutshell, is Tasha's formula for success. Should you happen to send any compliments in the direction of the peony beds, Tasha will insist that all the credit goes to the manure.

JUST A YEAR OR TWO AGO, Tasha got it into her head to create a garden specifically to accommodate her private artistic interludes. It was to be a hideaway replete with every sort of botanical conceit that she could possibly devise. Tucked in seclusion behind the henhouse, hemmed in by a ring of tall lilacs, which artfully disguise an electric fence to keep the deer at bay, the garden can only be discovered if you take a well-camouflaged path lined with forget-me-nots. Tasha calls it, quite appropriately, her secret garden.

The secret garden is a confection of all of Tasha's favorite flowers. As a consequence, the moment the garden began to look spectacular it defeated its purpose entirely – the secret garden ceased to be her private sanctum. In June, when the giant foxgloves are standing fully six feet tall, Tasha can never resist showing off their speckled spires. After she has toured all the terraces, she pauses just a

Weeding is a constant chore, and one that Tasha insists on performing herself. Certain meanderers, such as forget-me-nots and poppies, are allowed to seed themselves in. But the equally aggressive jewelweed is gingerly removed and carried to the compost pile.

moment before leading you through the well-concealed entryway. She'll stand beside those gigantic crowns of bells, beaming from ear to ear, and boast, "When I uncovered the foxgloves, they looked like weak celery. Now the blossom stalks are so thick that I can hardly put my hands around them." Again, manure came to the rescue. If you happened to visit in early spring, you would undoubtedly catch Tasha lugging bucket after bucket of manure tea over to her foxgloves and watering the fertilizer in.

In the center of the secret garden stands a gigantic flowering crab apple surrounded by a hexagonal bench built by Seth. With her usual sense of drama and design, Tasha put in a daring heart-shaped bed around the bench. But the profuse plantings (encouraged by copious fertilizer, of course) so quickly overspilled their boundaries that the original shape is no longer readily apparent. Although the garden lost its contours, the thick cover was its saving grace. Just a few years ago, this garden was a confusion of brambles. Overplanting has thwarted its desire to return to that independent state.

The secret garden is still in its infancy. Tasha always claims that it takes twelve years to make a good garden, so she has almost a decade of bending and shaping to accomplish before it reaches its zenith. Still, it has some delightful elements. In particular, the roses already look absolutely ravishing.

Richard took such a shine to Tasha's **Rosa 'William Baffin'** *that he snitched a cutting for his own garden. "Well, it's one of the few dependable climbers that we can grow up here," he'll say defensively when teased about his fondness for the shrub.*

Roses are a passion for Tasha, so it's little wonder that she put some especially aromatic David Austin hybrids at the entryway of her secret garden. She talks incessantly about these roses; they're the apple of her eye. When the snow isn't deep enough in winter, it's her 'Heritage' rose that she frets about. When summer seems far away, it's her 'Mary Webb' rose that she dreams of: "You should see her in June, she has the most delicate lemony yellow color coupled with an absolutely divine aroma." Although Tasha is fond of anything with a past, she is quick to accept the labors of modern craftsmen who share her standards of excellence, and she definitely sees David Austin as a craftsman – and a genius as well. She'll call up, all in a fluster, to say, "Have you seen David Austin's newest book? Why, it's ingenious. He plants his roses in groups of three, can you imagine it? So that's exactly what I plan to do from now on." Tasha is a perennial student.

THE SECRET GARDEN is not the only place where roses flourish. In fact, roses are everywhere on the property. As you wander in the labyrinth of winding paths around the terraces, you must continually bend this way and that to avoid being scalped by rose arbors encroaching on the walkway. Tasha collects legendary roses such as 'Maiden's Blush', 'York and Lancaster', 'Königin von Dänemark', and *Rosa canina*, chosen for their scents and their stories. Each is conscientiously planted in a spot protected from bitter gales, except a stupendous 'New Dawn' rose that runs along the fence beside the goat barn: "She gets the full brunt of the northwest wind, but she endures it, and she never gets mildew."

At one time Tasha was bent on constructing a formal rose garden leading into the vegetable beds. But the heirloom roses despised the damp soil, and the bricks that were laid for a pathway heaved and chipped pitifully, so the project was abandoned. To overcome her disappointment, she recently put in a bed of Bourbon roses riding the crest of the upper terrace. Every winter they're heaped with a mound of ancient sawdust mixed with urea to prevent the mulch from leaching nitrogen from the soil. "It looks like a little Egypt out there, really, with a line of pyramids," says Tasha.

In June, however, it's quite a different story. The roses emerge from their sawdust heaps quite resplendent, to unfold blossom after blossom in sheer gratitude. And Tasha, for her part,

In June, Tasha's fairy ring of dianthus opens, to encircle a tuffet of campanulas. Like everything in Tasha's world, the fairy ring is pure fantasy.

wanders about burying her nose in their petals, passing judgment on their perfumes, and complimenting their discreet colors and fine form. When the subject is roses, Tasha can talk by the hour, sharing her victories, probing to discover some little tidbit about care and cultivation that she might not already know. If she fails with a rose, she stubbornly tries again.

Perhaps I'm wrong, but sometimes it seems that Tasha holds the deepest affinity for the world's most finicky plants.

Daisy Garlands & Delphiniums

✤

AS YOU MAY HAVE GATHERED by now, Tasha is an uncommonly industrious soul. And time has scarcely put a brake to her unceasing momentum. Certainly, she's not averse to sitting down for a nice long chat. But she prefers to have something in her hands while discussing life, liberty, and lupines. In July, more often than not, you'll find Tasha on the porch overlooking her terraces, holding forth before a spellbound assemblage of friends and relatives. You'll find her sitting there with corgyn at her feet, spinning stories of her grandfather, who laid a heavy bet that peaches could be grown in Nahant, Massachusetts, and eventually won that wager. You'll find her telling tales – mostly true, some slightly embroidered, perhaps – with a half-smile playing on her lips. And all the while her fingers will be working, busily weaving daisy chains from the bounty in her meadow.

> " It's gardening and fresh goats' milk that keep me going. "

The meadow, the first sight that visitors behold as they drive onto the property, is a not-so-subtle hint that a gardener is in residence. But more than that, it provides a buffer zone between the all-too-real world outside and Tasha's 250 acres of sheer fantasy. I've sometimes wondered if Tasha would have planted right up to the road if her driveway weren't so very long. But I think not. Tasha likes the mile or more of wooded no man's land between her and the world.

The beauty of the meadow lies in its simplicity. After all, such a meadow could come as sheer accident. It could all be a delightful caprice of nature, since lupines and daisies grow here and there, seemingly of their own accord, in this neck of the woods. They seem to sprout unbidden, but Tasha will tell you that Alexander Graham Bell was responsible for planting all the wild lupines in New England from an arsenal of seed he carried in his pocket at all times. Like Johnny

Appleseed, he scattered them around everywhere he went. She knows that for a fact, because she played with his daughters as a child.

But of course the meadow was carefully planned and planted, and if it looks totally natural, that's all part of the ruse. Originally, the field had pathetically poor soil. "Oh, it was sad, really sad, lots of hardpan and pine trees," Tasha will reminisce. "Fifty years before I came, they raised potatoes on it, and that's all it was good for." So Tasha didn't really have to wrest the field from weeds when she decided to plant a meadow. She tilled it up and then went out with her bag of wildflower seed. That's when the convenient tourist showed up and finished the job — but I've already told that story.

B UT THERE'S MORE to the meadow saga than just the tale of how the fellow came to sow the seed. The meadow is expansive, although when you're driving up through the clouds of flowers, the masses of color shrink the perspective. "It must be three or four acres wide, don't you think?" Tasha will say, partly to herself or to anyone who might be within earshot. "But I'm terrible at judging distance. Mind you, I originally bought enough seed for two acres, and it only covered half the field." Anyway, after the seed was sown, Seth went out and rolled it — and that is Tasha's secret for success with wildflower meadows. "Well, I noticed that wildflower seed always comes up most

thickly where I've trod. So I thought that I'd give the rolling theory a chance. I've never had to sow the meadow again," Tasha says, with more than a little pride in her voice.

Beginning in late June, the field is dominated by the purple spires of lupines, and the display usually tarries well into July, depending on the weather, of course — lupines peter out quickly in heat. The meadow, the lupines, and their greater glory are all constant issues for Tasha and the grist for many stories. Since the meadow runs right up to the driveway, it is inevitably affected by the outside world, and Tasha must continually protect it from the trespasses of society. As you can well imagine, she usually comes out victorious.

Most critically, there's the issue of snow cover. Tasha is absolutely certain that snow is beneficial to lupines. And she has observed that the purple spires are most plentiful along the edge of the meadow, where the snowplow makes its piles. So in this one instance, Tasha and technology are on the same side. However, during one unfortunate winter, not only did the plowman fail to pile the snow properly, but he ventured past his prescribed boundaries and onto the meadow's turf. "Well, I was on the phone faster than you can wink an eyelash, I can assure you," Tasha still sputters. "And I told him in no uncertain

Although the oxeye daisies predominate in Tasha's meadow, oats, black-eyed Susans, soapwort, clover, vetch, and orchard grass are sprinkled about.

terms that I was not amused. He was most remorseful and gave me a year's worth of free plowing. Eventually, I accepted his apologies . . . with the strict understanding that it would never happen again."

THE MEADOW'S SPLENDOR goes far beyond the duration of the lupines. In fact, Tasha prefers the next step in the progression. When the lupines are just slightly past prime, the daisies begin, and the meadow slowly slips into a medley of oxeye daisies (*Chrysanthemum leucanthemum*) and dame's rocket (*Hesperis matronalis*). The combination of the yellow-and-white daisies and the lavender spikes of rocket pleases the artist beyond words. And later still come drifts of St. Johnswort, yellow clover, black-eyed Susan, and echinacea. At one time Shirley poppies dwelled in the field, but they couldn't compete with their more aggressive bedfellows, so they disappeared. Wild strawberries ("the sweetest I've ever tasted," boasts Tasha) grow in the acid soil at the upper end of the field, far away from the snowplow's caprices.

Apparently, the meadow requires little maintenance beyond the occasional friendly discussion with snow removal folks. For the sake of the daisies, Tasha throws around potash by the bucketful from her hard-working woodstove, and also spreads the ash from the annual midsummer bonfire. No other fertilizer is furnished. Punctually in mid-September of every year, Andy Rice, a neighbor, mows the field, and that's really the sum total of care that the meadow receives. For all that, it looks ravishing at any given moment – and it supplies Tasha with more than enough material for daisy garlands.

If there's a special occasion afoot – a wedding or the midsummer party – Tasha feels compelled to provide every youngster in attendance with a daisy crown. If a celebration is not on the docket, no matter; she weaves garlands anyway for the benefit of her grandchildren, secretly hoping that they're watching her hands and learning the ropes. Of course, she'll brush away compliments with an impatient, "Oh, I don't make proper wreaths, you know." And yet they look lovely and last quite a while. She soaks them in a pie plate ("or in the bathtub, if there's more than half a dozen") to extend their life. "But take care to shake them out before putting them on someone's head. I've had a few dozen little girls rushing around and squealing at the top of their lungs when the cold water dribbled down the back of their necks. Very disruptive."

Tasha's favorite spot for such creative endeavors is the upper terrace – in the shade of the porch in sunny weather, or out on the grass when the sunrays aren't so intense. Since the house is perched on top of a hill, the land flows down from the front door at a rather rakish angle: "Oh, you should have seen it before the terraces were put in. There was a sheer drop of about twelve feet straight down from the front door." Well, Tasha heard that Jim Herrick was among the best stonemasons in the territory, and she secured a promise that he would come by and remedy the situation. But time marched on and the mason didn't materialize, so Tasha decided to take

---

Tasha will protest that her wreaths are "nothing special," but they hold together splendidly, even though they are merely woven in and out and secured with thread.

matters into her own hands. She drew up a large poster and hung it in a conspicuous spot at the post office. It offered a generous reward for anyone who would deliver Jim Herrick to her front door (stone-laying tools in hand, of course). "What was the reward?" I wondered. "Why, a lemon meringue pie." He showed up the very next day with young Jimmy, his son, and they laid some of the best stone terraces in the county.

BUT THERE'S MORE to the terraces than clever stonework. As Tasha labors over her daisy chains, she overlooks a truly divine scene. All the terraces are rather dense with flowers at any given moment – that's Tasha's style. But she has outdone herself on the upper terrace, I think. The corgyn, when they romp, nearly disappear beneath clouds of white valerian (often called garden heliotrope, although the scent can't compare, in my opinion), lady's mantle, thalictrum, fragrant roses, fragrant alyssum, and fragrant cinnamon pinks. Nepeta runs everywhere, and lamb's ears edge the beds. Delphiniums stand majestically against the wall, and a colony of Tasha's own select strain of lettuce poppies, broadcast rather unceremoniously each year with a flick of the wrist out the back door, glistens in the sun. As if the beds weren't thick enough, Tasha keeps close by a clutch of urns and antique terra-cotta pots overflowing with favorite annuals, such as verbena, geraniums (pelargoniums, that is), pansies, genuine

Not everyone is fond of valerian, but Tasha insists that it's "a fine old herb, and I rather like the scent," so clouds of valerian frame her view of the lower terraces.

heliotrope, and petunias. There's a polite nod toward formality with twin pots of miniature pink 'The Fairy' roses beside a matched pair of miniature yellow 'Rise 'n' Shine' roses, all trained into standard-shaped topiary. But the nod is mostly tongue-in-cheek – the scene is such a delightful chaos that the containers simply add another voice to the bedlam. They sort of disappear beside the Shasta daisies, tall irises, and spires of *Sidalcea* balanced by white dragonhead (*Physostegia*) not far away. I could go on, I could fill page after page listing all the blossoms that surround Tasha as she sits and weaves, but I think you get the picture.

The beauty of it all is that everything seems to work together so harmoniously. ("Of course the colors combine," the artist will say, with just a hint of impatience. "Anything that fails to blend is not suffered to stay another moment.") In fact, I suspect that Tasha does a great deal of digging up and carting off to more tasteful locations when no one is looking. What remains is absolutely perfect.

From her perch on the upper terrace, Tasha has a good view of everything below. She can survey most of the middle and lower terraces and enjoy the overall picture of their progress and profusion. For a closer look, she wanders

Tasha can tell a story about nearly every vine on the premises. If asked to identify the blue clematis by the house, she'll respond, "Ah yes, that's 'Ramona'. I bought it from a funny old boy; I think he's since gone to heaven."

along one of her paths and down some very steep, very tight steps, escorted by an adoring contingent of corgyn. Tasha always moves quite effortlessly through the terrace labyrinth, despite bare feet and flowing skirts. The rest of humanity, however, has problems navigating the contours. The network of pathways is so much like a maze and so dense with blossoms that by mid-summer several corridors are completely hidden. But that's half the fun. Children and pets are in their glory; they disappear down steps and aren't seen again for hours, although you can occasionally hear delighted giggles filtering up through the flora.

I suppose that certain adults might not approve of Tasha's pathways. After all, they're sunken and nearly lost in banks of blossoms, and they're obstructed here and there by overzealous arbors. In fact, quite often, while traversing a chosen path and blindly following its convolutions, you will find a particularly wicked rose whipping you in the ankles or tangling in your hair. Generally speaking, though, the kind of people who wouldn't enjoy the terraces and their pranks are not prone to pay a visit. People who can't tolerate some tangled tresses and a snag or two are simply not among Tasha's friends.

Needless to say, the vines and their exuberance are totally intentional. Tasha has an affinity for vines; she can sympathize with their headstrong freedom and mischievous ways. When she first came, she planted vines

liberally wherever a climbing plant might find opportunity, and over the years she has added vines at every turn. Every trellis has its adoring vine weaving in and out. A honeysuckle

---

Vines interweave shamelessly beside Tasha's front door. Here an old lilac, Rosa *'Mme. Hardy', and* Clematis *'Jackmanii' form a delightful tangle (left). At the height of summer, irises open along the walls, taking the place where daylilies once reigned (above).*

and a *Clematis tangutica* enjoy a passionate love affair while furnishing shade over the arbor where Tasha used to take tea. A confusion of fragrant autumn-blooming *Clematis paniculata* climbs the porch with a self-seeding morning glory tangled in its leaves. A wisteria scrambles over the eaves where the doves set, and another wisteria embraces the patio where the cat naps. Rambling and climbing roses are allowed to wander wherever they might. Some arch gracefully, unsupported but framing a view

When it's necessary to stake the stately delphiniums, Tasha often secures them to the wall instead of running an unsightly stake up each spire. Here they stand with Maltese cross (Lychnis chalcedonica) *and peonies.*

before the path plummets down steps; others disguise frameworks that they long ago overcame. Another of Tasha's ploys is to let vines mingle with and embrace shrubs. The lilacs by the house have clematis threaded through their foliage, and the roses often are so coupled with clematis that you cannot tell where one vine begins and the other ends.

ALTHOUGH TASHA PROTESTS vigorously against the idea of choosing favorites and will rarely admit to favoring one plant over another, she definitely seems to gravitate toward clematis. And I suspect her predilection has something to do with the fact that these are replete with individual whims and fancies, and thus they provide the master gardener with a challenge. Each must be pruned at just the right moment; those that bloom on new growth should be clipped in early spring, those that flower on old wood are pruned in summer, and the very lethargic types aren't pruned at all. In general, Tasha doesn't prune vines arbitrarily. In fact, I've never seen her take a

pair of clippers to anything just to tidy it up in midseason. Beyond the pruning chores, there's clematis's penchant for cool roots but sunny branches to contend with. But as you can imagine, Tasha has a solution: "A flat rock at the base works like a charm."

JULY IS DENSE in Tasha's garden – dense with blossoms and thick with duties. Every year brings a different set of problems to be dealt with and dispatched. Some years, Tasha is busy battling the torrential thunderstorms that buffet her little mountaintop and wreak havoc on her stately spires of delphiniums, hollyhocks, and foxgloves. Tasha despises thunderstorms.

Apparently, her mother once came so close to being struck by lightning that all the bobby pins holding up her long tresses melted, giving her quite a fright. So Tasha has a healthy respect for storms, or, as she quips, quoting Mark Twain, "Thunder is impressive, but it's lightning that does the work." And of course the rain that accompanies the flashes and noise does a nasty job on the garden.

But more often than not, July is a month of drought, and that rankles the gardener even more than a few brief episodes of electrical terror. She fears for her lily pond; she fears for her shallow-rooted azaleas and the tender herbs that wilt on her terraces. "At fourteen hundred feet up, everything goes

While lunch is still baking, Tasha often sends visitors wandering down to witness the water lilies in their glory.

into a dead wilt at high noon," Tasha will mumble while wielding a truly immense long-spouted watering can. "If ever I had an enemy, I'd make him deal with my hoses. The moment I imagine that I finally have them straightened out, they thwart me." But in some years she dares not even use hoses, because the well is so low. Then Tasha nervously gravitates toward the pantry every few minutes, to put on her reading glasses and flick the barometer with her thumb,

shaking her head and sighing. "It's still steady on – we'll have no rain this afternoon."

The pond provides the most dramatic documentation of a drought. Usually it is dappled with fragrant water lilies in July. There is such a bounty that Tasha wades out, picks a few blossoms, and floats them in tubs indoors. Rebecca, her naughtiest corgi, ate every last cut water lily one year. But perhaps as a result of the ensuing bellyache or perhaps because of Tasha's firm reprimands, she never repeated the folly.

Recently, the dry summers have yielded precious few water lilies. Last year Richard arrived with his camera and tripod at dawn and, finding no one about, moseyed on down

to the lily pond. Heaven knows, Richard is not easily spooked. But Tasha says that when he returned, his face was one of sheer horror, and his voice still sounds incredulous when he describes what he found: "It looked as if someone had pulled the plug. It was gone,

"I must have the water lilies close by, so I swim them in tubs and washbasins and chamberpots, if need be," Tasha says.

empty, disappeared." It turned out that Tasha had scooped up the water lilies that her son Tom had sent for her birthday and taken them indoors to spend July and August floating in a bathtub. Fortunately, late summer brought a superabundance of precipitation, and the pond was ready to receive its flora again not many weeks thereafter. And it's a good thing, too, because I'm not sure how long Rebecca could resist the temptation of water lilies so close at hand.

Lilies & Berries to Spare

HAVE YOU EVER NOTICED that gardeners sometimes let things slip into oblivion in August? Weary of the tempo, tired of the unrelenting work that gardening entails, or perhaps slightly bored with summer's profusion, they let their gardens disintegrate into late-season scruffiness. But not Tasha. Her growing season is so brief that she savors every moment. The garden is almost as striking in August as it is in May.

Of course, Tasha would deny that she seeks out plants specifically to extend the growing season. She doesn't like to be caught in the act of deliberate planning. Yet I am fairly certain that she combs catalogues searching for things that might fill pauses in her garden. Apparently her search has been fruitful. To be sure, the garden looks different in midsummer than it did in spring. The beds are no longer a profusion of tight little clumps crowned with neat tufts of bloom. Instead, they have evolved into a

> " Why don't you show yourself around the garden while I fix tea? "

blowzy affair, a divine confusion of daisies, lilies, cleomes, feverfew, hollyhocks, and every other summertime bloomer that will endure Tasha's hilltop. The garden has become a riot of color.

Even in August, it's never terribly hot on Tasha's little mountain. I figure that the temperature must be at least five degrees cooler than the reading on the thermometer in town. But it can become rather dry and breezy at that elevation, and drought takes its toll. Tasha will do everything in her power to give plants whatever their little hearts desire as far as soil, shelter, and light are concerned. But she cannot meddle with the weather.

So the frantic pace calms a bit by August. First of all, there isn't much new business to address in the garden. High summer is not anyone's favorite moment to plant or transplant. In fact, you'll only find Tasha digging holes in August if someone has

brought a little rarity that simply must go into the ground posthaste. "Here," I'll say, handing her a pot of blue corydalis that I found in Britain, "slip this into some sunny spot." After Tasha has thanked me profusely and inquired about the plant's eccentricities and desires, she goes off, only to return with a rather impressive earth-moving tool. Not till then will she mention what must have been weighing on her mind for many minutes: "You know that I never, ever slip anything into the soil. When I plant, I use only a good stout shovel." And she proceeds to dig a hole.

EVEN THOUGH she might not be planting, there are plenty of chores to perform, and Tasha spends her time walking the paths, back and forth, up and down, with bundles of fruit or vegetables wrapped in her apron. "There is never a basket on hand when you need one," she'll mutter as she gathers plums into the folds of a billowing smock. Which brings us to the subject of her attire.

Tasha is always well clad. I have visited the garden on days when most mortals might be tempted to minimize their apparel. Richard will show up with rolled-up shirtsleeves, and I might have on only a slip of a sundress. Tasha, though, always has both her shoulders and her elbows completely covered, and her skirts flow nearly to her ankles. In very hot weather, she adds to the bulk by tying one

Tasha usually has plenty of all-too-eager help when harvesting, and not all the raspberries manage to find their way to the pantry. The corgyn are not above begging for raspberries, and have been known to help themselves.

scarf over her coiled braids and tucking another around her collar. As a matter of principle, she does not expose much skin to the elements. However, from springtime onward, she always wanders around the garden in bare feet. It's a habit that began in childhood, rumor has it, and ever since she has padded around barefoot when weather permits. Every once in a while, you'll hear her mumble, "Bother – I've just stepped on a bee." Expecting that she'll need some assistance, you rush to her side. But Tasha pauses only long enough to remove the offending insect from its target before proceeding undaunted on her way.

TASHA ENTERTAINS VISITORS during every month of the year, but friends seem to be particularly drawn to her cool mountaintop in August, and she is always the model hostess. Most especially, she likes to thrill company with goodies that she has baked with the harvest of the land. No matter how torrid the weather happens to be, Tasha fires up the woodstove if visitors are at hand. "I cook everything on my woodstove," she'll say with pride in her voice. "Of course, woodstoves are temperamental things. You have to use certain wood – you can't bake properly on pine and wood scraps. But I can successfully bake an angel cake now, and you know that isn't easy." Needless to say, Richard finds plenty of excuses to meander down to Tasha's at just this time of year. And Tasha loves to tease him about his appetite: "The last time he came unannounced, I told him that we'd just eaten the pie – all in jest, of course. His face fell a mile. He looked so crestfallen that I just had to bake him a pie that very moment." The truth is that Tasha dotes on Richard's discerning palate. Her cheeks light up with a golden glow whenever he peeks through the door and ventures to say hopefully, "Something smells good . . ."

When Tasha treks down the terraces to fetch produce for her culinary projects, she encounters plenty of diversion along the way. The garden really is resplendent with blooms. Because everything has gained height and lushness at this time of year, the terraces seem suffused with bright color, unlike the timid hues of spring. The flowers are more assertive now, like the open-faced echinacea petals and the plump hollyhocks that line the paths. ("Oh, I just love hollyhocks, but only the singles, mind you – I won't look twice at the doubles.") The hollyhocks seem to seed themselves in, and they do wonderful things, come midsummer. Their stalks are lined with a plethora of blossoms in sweet pastels, and my eyes fill with ill-concealed envy whenever I pass them by. Not a leaf is tattered by Japanese beetles; it's just too cold in Tasha's garden for those pests to survive a winter.

If I am jealous of Tasha's hollyhocks, I

When forced to choose a favorite, Richard admits that he prefers raspberry pies above all. When Tasha hears that he's about to arrive, she fires up the woodstove, no matter how hot it happens to be outdoors.

nearly perish with envy over her sweet peas. The cool summers on the hilltop nurture the finest sweet peas that I have ever beheld. Of course, the weather cannot take full credit for

"Remember, you've promised to share some of your black hollyhocks from Monticello," Tasha may say. "But my favorites are still the melon-colored seedlings" (above). Not far away is a tangle of sweet peas from Agway, blossoming in raging shades (left).

the crop; Tasha puts considerable effort into the extravaganza every year. There must be some sort of competition going on between Tasha and her neighbors, since they are all vying to produce the first and finest sweet-pea flowers in their neck of the woods. Tasha tries to get a jump on the other contenders by rushing into Agway in winter to buy the seed that has just arrived, soaking the peas overnight, rolling them in an inoculant of nitrogen-fixing bacteria, and planting them in peat pots set on her bedroom windowsill. In

Although Steve Davie mows the fields, there are places where Tasha wouldn't let a man loose with a scythe. She cuts around her precious hollyhocks herself, then carefully rakes the trimmings.

spring, she plants them out next to a wire fence in the vegetable garden and digs a trench alongside the young vines. As the sweet peas stretch, the trench receives frequent applications of manure tea, which Tasha brews in a huge covered caldron kept far off the beaten path. Efner, Tasha's daughter, brings her cow flops in spring especially for this purpose; they are thrown into the barrel, water is added, and the whole murky mess stews for the remainder of the summer. "It's not a particularly fragrant affair," Tasha will warn before removing the lid and ladeling out a gallon to dilute with a gallon of water and slosh into the sweet-pea ditch. As it turns out, her warning is the understatement of the century. Still and all, that malodorous mixture nurtures the tallest ("they go up seven feet, some of them"), most aromatic sweet peas I've ever encountered. After being showered with leading compliments, Tasha usually sends me home with a generous bouquet of these winged flowers.

A LTHOUGH TASHA'S PROPERTY might be cooler than land down below, it can still get quite toasty in midsummer, especially if you have just helped get the woodstove going. In August, Tasha sends visitors down to the pond, not only to see the water lilies but also to paddle about. She might follow with her Austrian scythe to manicure the grass around the japonica

primroses not far from the water's edge. "Oh, I wouldn't trust a man to cut around my primroses," she explains. "And I'm quite handy with the scythe, really." But even when she happens to be in that general vicinity, she never goes swimming: "I come from a sea-faring family. After all, Mama was one of the first women to get her pilot's license, to navigate Papa's boat. But I've never liked water. I think I have some cat in me, actually."

One cannot possibly visit Tasha in August and fail to be impressed by her lilies. "I'm not very knowledgeable about lilies," she will say, brushing away inquiries as to her secrets for success. Her favorites ("I have some real stunners") are sheltered by the terrace's eight-

Tasha is especially fond of her 'Imperial Silver' lilies, which raise tall spires of blossoms but last only two weeks. When she has an abundance, the blooms go into flower arrangements, keeping company with cleomes, baby's breath, echinacea, and Queen Anne's lace.

foot stone wall. *Lilium regale*, 'Black Dragon', and some equally ravishing oriental hybrids send up spires of majestic blooms to perfume the air in late summer. Not only does the wall buffer "the wicked northwest wind," but Jim Herrick's meticulously placed stones also store heat on sunny days to moderate the temperature drop at nightfall. Furthermore, a fine stand of Asiatic lilies graces the edges of the peony garden, picking up the thread after the peonies have dropped their final petals.

Although daylilies ought not to be mentioned in the same breath as genuine lilies, in late summer you cannot help but notice that a few hemerocallis crouch at the bottom of Tasha's lowest terrace. Once upon a time a whole brigade of them lined the wall, but Tasha moved them elsewhere: "Daylilies are raggedy, don't you think?" And off they went.

Besides coddling the lilies in the garden, Tasha has taken to growing lilies in pots as well, to be trundled anywhere she feels that a few impressive trumpets are needed. Usually they preside over tea on the porch. She plants them in autumn, covers the pots with mesh ("so the mousies don't indulge"), and stashes them in the cellar until sprouts appear in January. Then they go into a shaded nook of the greenhouse. By July, they're in full fanfare.

THE FLOWERS ARE ALL well and good, but being a proper Yankee, Tasha has a practical bent. The garden is sprinkled everywhere with fruit trees and berries of various descriptions. No doubt

Tasha mingles the oversized flowers of her tall 'Black Dragon' trumpet lilies with pink 'Parisienne' and yellow 'Ballard' Asiatic lilies. As filler, she loves to use the buttonlike blossoms of her heirloom single feverfew.

in her eyes they give the place integrity. And yet every fruit-bearing bush is cushioned with flowers. Quite literally, the garden offers food for both body and soul.

I can't think of a berry or fruit that Tasha hasn't tried somewhere on her 250 acres. Of course, prudence dictates some of her selections. There's absolutely no point in growing tender fruits that will not survive the terrors of a New England winter. Still, she harbors an apricot tree in the protective ell of the house. She has never picked an apricot yet, but the tree hasn't perished, either, and as she often says, "Hope springs eternal in the human breast."

Peaches are another story entirely. Lining the steps down to the vegetable garden are several very impressive 'Reliance' peach trees, all laden with fruit, and Tasha is more than a little proud of their performance. 'Reliance' was developed by Elwyn Meader, a professor at the University of New Hampshire – "an awfully nice person," Tasha says. "He had so many apricots in his northern garden that we used to sit under the trees and become quite full just eating the drops. Mine will produce like that someday." Anyone who has ever eaten a peach knows that all hybrids are not equally tasty. But Elwyn Meader's peach is scrumptious. "Those fruits are delicious," Richard confides. "Don't tell Tasha, but I've

been known to forage among them." I don't think he has her fooled for a moment.

There are other fruits to tempt Richard. Although Tasha insists that she prefers the little wild blueberries that grow by the road-side for muffins and whatnot, she keeps a few token bushes of the fatter hybrid berries for eating with goat cream (she has her own cream separator, a mighty gadget composed of a million rings which must all be washed and dried after use). Surplus blueberries are frozen or bottled in light syrup for winter. Raspberries, in contrast, are made into jam, especially the crops that bedeck the canes of 'Latham' and 'September Gold'. "The very best are the black raspberries," Tasha opines. "But you have to add apples to make the jam set, because they don't have sufficient pectin."

The raspberries must be pruned, of course, and that's always a major issue. Pruning should be performed in January, but the snow is invariably too deep to accomplish the deed. But Tasha doesn't worry: "I've read of a new method of pruning the bearing stems in autumn, and I'm itching to try it."

BEYOND THE BERRIES, apples, plums, and pears are planted not far from the vegetable garden. The pear tree's identity is a mystery. It came with Tasha from a past home, and she probably knew its name once, but it has since slipped from her

Although Tasha picks pounds of wild blueberries for baking, she keeps several cultivated bushes for enjoying with cream and serving to company.

memory. Anyway, it was transplanted not by virtue of its fine fruit but because its silhouette was so comely that the artist simply could not leave it behind. Still, Tasha insists that the fruit bottles superbly when it finally ripens up.

Tasha is a fan of Elwyn Meader's 'Reliance' peach, specially bred to produce in a northern garden. Unlike the blueberries, the peaches never seem to find their way into pies.

The plums, on the other hand, are acclaimed for their crop rather than their contours. Tasha has a couple of yellow plums on the southeast slope stretching down from the greenhouse. Their fruits are so delectable that even the corgyn snitch whatever they can pilfer by standing on their hind legs and pulling limbs down. Tasha tries her best to prevent the thievery – "After all, plums give them a terrible case of the trots" – but I've caught them in the act on more than one occasion.

THE FRUIT TREES ENTICE visitors down to the vegetable garden, which harbors broccoli, kale, tomatoes, peas, beans, cabbage, brussels sprouts, lettuce, spinach, and "all the usual things," and a fine crop of flowers as well. There's a philosophy behind it, or so Tasha claims. "I think that plants prefer some sort of undergrowth to keep their roots damp," she will explain while pushing her way past the daisies, dill, poppies, and calendulas that have sown themselves in or taken root around the beanpoles. Of these volunteers, only the dill has a good excuse for being in a vegetable patch. Yet it all appears so very fine and the harvest is so impressive that no one dares to look askance.

Although the vegetable garden is not the first place that Tasha will take visitors when they arrive, she is mighty proud of its produce. Mostly she values the garden for its contribution to her menu. The peas, however, are treasured for their beauty as well as their yield. Tasha grows 'Thomas Laxton' peas, those gigantic telephone-pole vines that stretch to seven feet if given the opportunity. In spring, she plants lettuce between the rows to conserve space. Not content merely with an early-season display, she puts in a second crop in late July or August, when the weather isn't too steamy, to be harvested in September. She grows scarlet runner beans because Thomas Jefferson did likewise, although she confesses that the taste of her 'Kentucky Wonder' pole beans is far superior. And of course she tries melons, garlic, and lima beans, which are bound to fail because of the short season. She dislikes pumpkin – "and I'm not mad about squash, either. But I'll eat it, if you insist." In this case she justifies her

prejudices by maintaining that pumpkins and winter squashes wouldn't have a long enough season to ripen, and maybe she's right.

So Tasha doesn't have many regrets about her northern garden and its cycles. For the most part, she has shaped her tastes to suit the climate or outsmarted the weather by careful

The vegetable garden hosts more than just culinary delights. Calendulas, which Tasha calls by their common name, pot marigolds, and dill, poppies, and daisies are also in residence. A morning glory shares a pole of the tepee with the scarlet runner beans. Although Tasha cannot grow some vegetables because of the cool climate, she harvests incredible cabbages.

planning. Certainly during some seasons the lack of precipitation rankles the gardener somewhat – especially in August; especially if the blueberries don't bear. And occasionally the early frosts cause her more than a little consternation, especially if they come in August. But by and large, when faced with New England's weather, Tasha thrives on it.

Gathering the Harvest

BESIDE TASHA'S TELEPHONE is a wall with dozens of names, numbers, and drawings scrawled on its surface. When Tasha wants to call someone, she walks over to the phone, puts on her reading glasses, and studies the wall, searching for the number in question. Actually, all sorts of information finds its way onto those weathered boards: names of nurseries, fertilizer formulas, Latin binomials, and sketches of adorable corgyn. But Tasha's most vital information is filed safely in her head.

Every now and then, I'll ask Tasha the name of a lily with an incredible scent or a pansy with lavender petals. She'll think a bit, tell a story or two about her Scottish nanny, and then usually come up with the identity of the mystery plant. However, if the name doesn't come to mind in the time it takes to spin several stories, she'll sigh and admit defeat — for the time being, anyway. "I'll have to look that up for you," she'll say. The truth is that she needs to search her memory in solitude.

Nonetheless, Tasha has a formidable horticultural library close at hand, filled with books that provide inspiration and advice. The room under the eaves and above the winter kitchen is completely given over to books; four shelves running the length of the walls groan beneath the weight of prodigious stacks of gardening volumes, both new and old. That is where Tasha disappears when she needs to know about the proper care and feeding of Parma violets or the whims and fancies of a certain heirloom rose. "It's not organized, you know," she'll say apologetically. "I tried to put it in order once, but it's quite impossible. There are simply too many volumes." Yet she seems to know approximately where everything is, especially her violet books, Emerson's *Trees and Shrubs of America*, and her mother's first editions of Gertrude Jekyll's writings. But sometimes you'll hear an "Oh, fiddle!" drifting down

> " We had a dandy frost last night. I had to cover the grape arbor with old laundry. "

from the second floor, and then you can be fairly certain that a sought-after volume is being elusive.

Naturally, Tasha's telephone wall has a complete list of all the friends and neighbors whom she might call upon in times of need. For the most part, Tasha prefers to perform the critical tasks of gardening herself, thank you. She has had gardeners in the past, but she is perhaps too independent-minded to have anyone else planning, planting, or transplanting in her garden. However, a few close

and trusted friends usually help with the back-breaking labor that might overly stress someone of her advanced years. "I have the best help, really," Tasha will say. "I couldn't ask for better, and we have lots of fun

Saffron crocus (Crocus sativus) adds autumn color to Tasha's garden. Meanwhile, she harvests the pears when they are still rock solid: "I don't know exactly which variety they are, but they ripen very late indeed."

Berries provide food for both Tasha and the birds. Barberries (Berberis vulgaris) go into jelly, while mountain ash berries feed winged friends.

together." Isabel Hadley, "who's a very learned herbalist," tackles some of the chores, and Melanie Boyd, "who spends many hot hours weeding," can often be found laboring somewhere on the property. Steve Davie, who does the scything with relish and gusto, is so good-natured that he'll claim to enjoy inhaling the essence of pigeon guano if Tasha hints that the coop requires cleaning. When it's necessary to wheelbarrow manure hither and yon, Andy Rice stops by, usually accompanied by his Border collie, much to the delight of Tasha's corgyn: "My Owen is usually such a social snob, you know, but he isn't too uppity to enjoy a good run with a pedigreed Border collie." Daughters, sons, and grandchildren often lend a hand, especially Winslow, Tasha's grandson who lives next door.

Winslow is the one Tasha calls on in September when she's ready to move the potted plants back into the greenhouse. At that point, they've spent the summer luxuriating in the garden, gaining the benefit of the crosswinds and the sunshine. Transporting them back inside is a mighty project, for sure, and every year the magnitude of the task increases in direct proportion to the quantity of manure tea that has been lavished on these plants in the interim. The bay tree in particular has become so bulky that Tasha now refers to the plant as "he." As I've mentioned, most plants are feminine in Tasha's eyes; even when speaking of the stout mock orange, she will say, "She takes up a generous corner of the greenhouse, you know." However, when the sweet bay was graduated into a half-barrel last summer and then wheeled back inside in autumn, Tasha called to report that "he has safely been removed to his winter quarters."

Tasha usually calls me only when some very rare violets have sprouted or when the heat goes off in her greenhouse. More often, I call her to ask advice about germinating primroses or to worry out loud about the health and welfare of my dairy goats. When Tasha picks up the phone, I am greeted by a chorus of barking. "Wait a minute while I silence the dogs," she'll say. I obediently hold my breath, listening to the stern "Shush!" at the other end of the line, and finally silence prevails. Only then does Tasha ask to whom she is speaking. We begin comparing the attributes and availability of heirloom pansy cultivars; time slips away, and before we know it, Tasha's dinner has nearly boiled dry or the stove needs more wood. Still, no matter how pressing her chores might be, she always finds a moment before hanging up to inquire, "What is the weather doing down there? I'm dying to know." Her weather is invariably doing something far more impressive. In fact, she's generally appalled at my lackluster weather reports from Connecticut.

In September, more often than not, the weather update concerns the arrival of a frost. Of course, Tasha's frosts come long before

Tasha can see a use for everything. In autumn she collects maple leaves – the brightest, biggest ones, of course – to store in the barn and feed to the goats in leaner times. The asters provide some interest for traveling monarch butterflies.

anyone else's. Sometimes her garden is nipped as early as August, but she usually forestalls the inevitable by throwing linens over her favorite tender plants on particularly chilly nights. The August scare happens now and then, but more frequently Tasha's garden is felled by a frost during the first week of September. "It's especially annoying when we are seared by a killing frost so early and then have

blissfully warm weather for another month or so," Tasha will grumble. But even when the tender plants have succumbed, many chores await. Tasha has a very highly developed squirreling instinct, and autumn is the time when her urge to prepare for leaner times gets plenty of exercise.

HAVE I MENTIONED that Tasha loves to harvest? She'll call up in autumn about something of major importance, such as the greening of pale camellia foliage or the eradication of some dreaded pest, but she'll always slip in a mention of the bushels of Concord grapes that she has just finished making into jelly. The grapes

would be ruined by frost, of course, but Tasha drapes the arbor with a sheet to shelter her precious crop. She thrives on jams and jellies, and makes apple jelly and raspberry, peach, blueberry, and black thimbleberry jams. ("The peach jam is delectable," Richard whispers under his breath when we are given a choice for tea.) Even the common barberries (*Berberis vulgaris*) that grow down by the azalea garden are boiled to make a tart jelly. Tasha herself couldn't possibly eat all those condiments, but she will use many of them to reward the hard labors of friends who come to visit over the next year, and she sends out a number of jars annually as highly coveted Christmas gifts. I suspect that the corgyn also crave a portion of the harvest, although Tasha will insist that she never succumbs to their begging for goodies. When Owen Corgyn fixes her with one of his long yearning looks, though, how can she resist?

Not all of Tasha's berries and fruits are meant to be harvested; she has planted several fruiting trees and bushes to lure and nourish the wild birds. The rose hips that set after the terrace ramblers blossom and the bright orange berries on the mountain ash ("In Scotland it's called the rowan, you know, and it's supposed to ward off witches") combine with the prodigious crop of crab apples to keep the birds well stocked throughout the winter months. In autumn, bluejays and cedar waxwings swarm over the crab apples in droves, and they are "truly contented birdies," as Tasha would say. But in late winter their delight reaches the plain of euphoria. Richard, who has witnessed the phenomenon, explains: "Well, they all get tight. By then the crab apples are fermented, and you can imagine the scene . . ."

Once I made the mistake of asking Tasha if she goes nut-collecting in the fall. Without pause, she responded, "I do not care for nuts," in such a resolute tone that I thought it best not to press the issue. To be sure, there are no nut trees on her property. However, although Tasha doesn't use nuts in cooking, she has been known to employ black walnut hulls and hickory husks to make dyes. Several years ago she found a piece of checked fabric jammed into a hole in her 1830 loom and copied it in wool using indigo, onion skins (which yielded a dove color), and black walnut hulls ("They make a lovely corgi color")

Until she can find the apple of her dreams, Tasha grows only a few trees on her property. In potatoes, Tasha prefers 'Green Mountain' and 'Katahdin', and thanks to the generous care and feeding that she lavishes on the potato field, the crop is fairly impressive each year.

as dyes. The dress that she stitched from that wool was her favorite for quite some time. But a gardener's clothing does not last long, and the dress ended up as a puppy bed when its service as a garment had finished.

THROUGHOUT THE SEASONS, Tasha's attire remains fairly constant. She always wears a print dress with long sleeves, a fitted bodice, and an ankle-length, flowing skirt. As the temperature drops, however, she adds layers. In autumn, the clothesline down by the azaleas dances with shawls, cloaks, and petticoats being aired in preparation for the coming chill. Tasha's red flannel petticoats and black woolen stockings keep her warm beneath, while several strata of shawls, each pinned on with a wonderful heirloom brooch, keep the drafts from her shoulders. As the season progresses, she dons one of her hooded cloaks before attending to chores outside. She really does look quite dashing, and just a tad eccentric, thus clad while digging potatoes in the fields.

For Tasha, potato digging is one of the high points of the year, an event certainly worthy of some fancy dressing: "I love to dig potatoes. It's quite satisfying, you know, like searching for buried treasure. Although it can be irksome when your spade slices a plump, promising potato in two." The naughty corgyn, always out for a lark, go running off with potatoes in their mouths and gnaw them ruthlessly to pieces before rushing back to steal more tuberous victims. But there are plenty of potatoes to spare, because Tasha spent long hours in the summer forking compost over the bed and hilling the fertile soil high around the stems of vines. "I'm crazy about potatoes — it must be my Irish ancestry," she'll confess to anyone who's good

enough to help her lug a heavy potato-heaped bushel basket into the root cellar.

The root cellar sees a lot of coming and going in autumn. The potato baskets are deposited in the dark, cool portion of the cellar just inside the door. Down the steps and further in the depths, Tasha stores crates of carrots, beets, and turnips layered in sand, which she sprinkles with water every once in a while. She has crates of leeks tied in bunches, and occasionally she hangs some cabbages, which she digs up by the roots, shakes free of soil, and ties around the neck with a string so they can dangle until needed. She doesn't always manage to eat all the cabbage heads before they spoil, but Tasha never wastes a leaf: "The spoils are fed to the hens." And that, in a nutshell, is Tasha's philosophy of life. Not a moment, not an action, not a leaf is ever wasted.

AUTUMN IS TRADITIONALLY apple season in New England, and Tasha can think of plenty of good uses for apples. She doesn't grow many on her own property, and Richard often complains that

Tasha can find a glorious bouquet anytime, and in fall her porch holds masses of autumn leaves, delphiniums, crab apples, and hydrangeas. At this time of year, when they can do little damage, the plump Brahmas and Cochins are allowed to wander.

those she does grow aren't conducive to casual snacking. But generous neighbors with large orchards provide Tasha with more apples than she can possibly use for jelly, cider, and apple-

Tasha is forever planting more bulbs, especially crocuses, "to thwart the greedy voles." By the time bulb-planting season has arrived, she has added several pounds of layers to her attire, and she often pulls a quilted petticoat over everything to keep warm.

sauce. Richard is particularly fond of the applesauce: "It's delicious. She serves it with a big glob of goat's-milk yogurt and crumbled sugar cookies. I know it sounds awful, but it's sublime."

Pears are more plentiful on Tasha's land. Since they cannot possibly ripen before killing frosts come, Tasha picks the crop when the fruits are still rock solid and ripens them safely inside. While they soften, she stores them upstairs, in the hallway and in the guest room. "People must pick their way into the

room through a maze of pears," she admits, "but really, it's the perfect ripening place." I'm sure that no one has ever complained.

WHILE FRUITS AND VEGETABLES are being harvested, bulbs are being planted. Every year Tasha increases her inventory of bulbs ("Well, I have to give the voles something to carry off each winter," she'll say in her own defense). So each spring the bulb extravaganza becomes a little more dramatic, and every autumn Tasha pulls on extra layers of woolies and marches out with her good stout trowel to plant bulbs.

I suspect that like her favorite writer, Mark Twain, Tasha occasionally stretches the truth

Hard frost might etch the ferns in a lovely hoar, but it takes its toll on the garden. Tasha always leaves the clinging crab apples for the birds, who delight in her generosity, especially when the fruit ferments into a fine mead.

just a bit when it comes to snow depths and wind-chill factors. But when she warns that she has "a shocking quantity" of bulbs to bury, she isn't exaggerating one iota. Fortunately for anyone who volunteers to help, Tasha doesn't bother to plant each bulb individually. If she did, we would be out there still. Instead, she digs troughs and nestles many bulbs in each furrow. "The trick is to fit

in the new ones and not disturb what has already been planted," she warns accomplices. When adding further delights to the ribbon of species tulips, *Iris reticulata*, and other bulbs that spill down the steps into the vegetable garden, she mumbles, "They should really invent a bulb detector for absent-minded gardeners such as myself."

In general, Tasha keeps an eye on the moon when planting anything. Being a naturalist at heart, she's quite aware of what's going on with the planets – their phases and conjunctions. Root crops such as carrots and potatoes are sown on a waning moon, while aboveground plants like the leafy herbs are planted under the waxing moon. "So into which category do crocuses fall?" I'll ask. "Whichever you like," she'll respond, in obvious high spirits because all the bulbs have been tucked safely below soil.

Speaking of herbs, the harvest from the herb garden just outside the greenhouse door should all be bunched, tied, and hung to dry in the attic by autumn. Herbs have always appealed to Tasha. At first I assumed it was their pretty foliage or perhaps their poignant pasts that piqued Tasha's interest. Now I'm fairly certain that she loves their usefulness – the fact that herbs alone combine utility and beauty in a single breath.

When Tasha and I met, years ago, herbs

"I believe in keeping warm," Tasha will say, and her house is always nice and toasty when the weather is chilly outside. To keep it that way, she collects kindling, accompanied by Minou, her one-eyed cat.

were our common ground. I was just beginning to explore herbs, and she knew them intimately. She was sculpting them into topiaries, combining them in ornamental planters, and mixing dried herbs into teas. Now, many of her potted herbs are thirty years old or more, and they look just splendid. The herb garden has reached a stunning state of maturity, with sage, marjoram, thyme, and chamomile coming up year after year and essential annuals such as summer savory and basil being replanted when the weather is warm. Tasha collects red clover from the meadow for tea, and she dries bay leaves from her massive specimen to give away to friends at Christmas. When Tasha sends one of her notes on Jenny Wren stationery, she invariably tucks a sprig of rosemary ("for remembrance") inside. And when I open my mailbox the aroma wafts out. Even before I slit open the envelope, I know who sent the note.

As September slips into October and autumn fades away, Tasha still has plenty of projects at hand. There are bulbs to be planted in pots if she's to have blossoms in the depths of winter, and there's goat cheese to be sprinkled with sage, pressed, waxed, and turned. The cold frame must be filled with pots of primroses and flats of pansy seed, and all must be covered with firm wire mesh to deter "those greedy rodents." Tasha once said to me,

As the season wends on, Tasha spends evening hours in her deacon's chair by the fire, with her work and some paperwhites close by. Often in winter she knits, sews, or mends; her hands are always busy, and her head is forever filled with dreams.

"Next year, I'm going to build myself a proper cold frame, mark my words, just like the one I saw in *The Tale of Benjamin Bunny*. Now that was a fine piece of craftsmanship, with stout brick sides." Can't you just see her leafing through the pages of Beatrix Potter's books, learning to be a better gardener, picking out ideas?

There are flats of violets to be sown and friends to call up when the seeds don't germinate with all due haste. There are evenings to sit by the fire with a corgi on her lap and read and worry about the snow depths. There are days when the snow is piled so high that Tasha can only guess what might be going on underneath: "I haven't seen a single mouse track this month. They must all be under the snow, eating my tulips." There is time to indulge in all kinds of cunning horticultural fantasies. Other gardeners might grow restless in November; they might curse the stubble-filled fields and whistling winds of New England. But not Tasha. After all, in November she can finally admire the structure of her fine stone terraces and dream of the blossoms that will completely overwhelm the stonework in a few brief months.

Some of Tasha's Favorite Nurseries

MAIL-ORDER NURSERIES

American Primrose Society

Addaline W. Robinson
9705 S.E. Spring Crest Drive
Portland, OR 97225
"I'm only a member of one plant society, and that's because I'm so fond of its seed list."

B & D Lilies

330 P Street
Port Townsend, WA 98368
206-385-1738
catalogue $3.00
"All the lilies in my garden have come from B & D."

Canyon Creek Nursery

3527 Dry Creek Road
Oroville, CA 95965
916-533-2166
catalogue $2.00
"Wonderful; this is where I get my heirloom dianthus."

Chiltern Seeds

Bortree Stile, Ulverston
Cumbria LA12 7PB, England
catalogue $4.00
"They have seeds of all sorts of little rarities."

Johnny's Selected Seeds

310 Foss Hill Road
Albion, ME 04910-9731
207-437-9294
catalogue free
"I always order my vegetable seeds from Johnny's because they're bred for a cold climate."

Logee's Greenhouses

141 North Street
Danielson, CT 06239
203-774-8038
catalogue $3.00
"Well, I've been getting dwarf fuchsias and rare pelargoniums from Logee's for ages."

Nuccio's Nurseries

P.O. Box 6160
3555 Chaney Trail
Altadena, CA 91003
818-794-3383
catalogue free
"I think they have excellent camellias."

Pickering Nurseries, Inc.

670 Kingston Road (Highway 2)
Pickering, Ontario L1V 1A6
Canada
416-839-2111
catalogue $3.00
"For old roses, they're tops."

Reath's Nursery

P.O. Box 247
County Road 577
Vulcan, MI 49892
906-563-9777
catalogue $1.00
"They have dandy peonies."

Southmeadow Fruit Gardens

15310 Red Arrow Highway
Lakeside, MI 49116
616-469-2865
catalogue free
"They list some very rare antique fruit trees you won't find elsewhere."

Van Engelen, Inc.

313 Maple Street
Litchfield, CT 06759
203-567-5662
catalogue free
"If you need large quantities of bulbs, they have quite reasonable prices."

~

NURSERIES TO VISIT

Allen Haskell

787 Shawmut Avenue
New Bedford, MA 02746
open 8-5, 7 days a week
"Oh, he has a nursery filled with lusty-looking topiaries."

Blanchette Gardens

223 Rutland Street
Carlisle, MA 01741
"They have lovely primulas and perennial geraniums."

Blue Meadow Farm

184 Meadow Road
Montague Center, MA 01351
"They have outstanding select perennials, such as meconopsis and an extraordinary array of morning glories."

Equinox Nursery

Manchester Center
Manchester, VT
"They have both perennials and annuals."